CRAIG CONLEY

ONE-LETTER WORDS

WORDS

A Dictionary

HarperCollins*Publishers*

Portions of the introduction first appeared in *Verbatim: The Language Quarterly* and are reprinted with permission.

ONE-LETTER WORDS: A DICTIONARY. Copyright © 2005 by Craig Conley. All rights reserved. Printed in the United States of America. No part of this book may be used or reproduced in any manner whatsoever without written permission, except in the case of brief quotations embodied in critical articles and reviews. For information, address HarperCollins Publishers, 10 East 53rd Street, New York, NY 10022.

HarperCollins books may be purchased for educational, business, or sales promotional use. For information, please write: Special Markets Department, HarperCollins Publishers, 10 East 53rd Street, New York, NY 10022.

FIRST EDITION

Designed by Matteo Bologna/Mucca Design

Printed on acid-free paper

Library of Congress Cataloging-in-Publication Data
Conley, Craig.
    One-letter words: a dictionary / Craig Conley.—1st ed.
        p.   cm.
ISBN 0-06-079873-4 (acid-free paper)
1. English language—Dictionaries. 2. One-letter words — Dictionaries. I. Title.
PE1680.C59   2005
423'.1—dc22   2005040547

05 06 07 08 09   ❖/RRD   10 9 8 7 6 5 4 3 2 1

For M. T. Wentz

The conquest of the superfluous gives us greater spiritual
excitement than the conquest of the necessary.
—Gaston Bachelard, *French philosopher*

ACKNOWLEDGMENTS

Thank You

Rana Bakhtiari, Firda Beka, Colleen Bell, John and Virginia Berland, Dan and Jan Bond, Wyman Brantley, Matt Brelje, Sheryl Burgstahler, John Burkardt, Tara Calishain, Alison Callahan, Jonathan and Hilary Caws-Elwit, Andrew Chorney, Steve Chrisomalis, Norris and Donna Clark, Ken Clinger, Allan and June Conley, Frank and Ramesh Conley, Bernie DeKoven, Dirk Dupon, Terry and Cathi Edward, Randy Fairbanks, Frank and Laura Farley, Frank Farley III, Kate Flannery, John K. Flynn, Ian Fraser, Reta Gardner, Charisse Gendron, Anne Greenshields, Judy Harwood, John Hilowitz, Sarah Houghton, Clark Humphrey, Ann Koupman, Blaire Larsen, Susan Larsson, Dave Lindner, Doug MacClure, Erin McKean, Jim and Glenda McKnight, Lindsay Marshall, Martin A. Mazur, Jeff Miller, Alice Obermiller, Fred O'Bryant, Edward J. Pelegrino, Carson Reynolds, Scot Robinson, Stuart Schwartz, Laurel Scott, Ivan Stang, Nancy Steele, John Walkenbach, Mike Warren, Michael Warwick, Ted Weinstein, Chris Winter, and Bev Yates.

INTRODUCTION

WHEN THE WORDS GET IN THE WAY

Ninety-nine down: a one letter word meaning
something indefinite.
The indefinite article or—would it perhaps be the
personal pronoun?
But what runs across it? Four letter word meaning
something
With a bias towards its opposite, the second letter
Must be the same as the one letter word.
It is time
We left these puzzles and started to be ourselves.
And started to live, is it not?
—Louis MacNeice, *Solstices*

We live in a world of mass communication. As you read this, words are staring *you* in the face. But they're not the only ones. Miles above you, words are flown in jets across the country and over the oceans. They are tossed at 5 a.m. on newspaper routes. They are delivered six days a week by mail carriers. They're propped up on display at book stores. They're bouncing off satellites and showing up on television and cell phone screens.

We are constantly bombarded by language pollution. And these empty words are overwhelming. Either they scream out to be noticed (as in TV commercials), or they hide in small print (at the bottom of contracts), or they bury their meaning behind jargon (generated by computers and bureaucracy).

It's enough to make you speechless.

Have you ever started to write a letter only to realize that you have nothing to report? "Dear Jan: Nothing exciting has happened here this month." No news may be good news, but it still doesn't amount to anything.

Sometimes you do have something to say, but "the words get in the way." You can't find the precise word for what you mean, and every word you can think of gives the wrong impression or is misleading.

The solution is to get back to basics. Put your trust in the ABC's. With this dictionary of one-letter words, you have the power to fight jargon and to simplify modern communication. It's now up to you.

THE SKINNY ON THE DICTIONARY OF ONE-LETTER WORDS

*"I'll tell you a secret—I can read words of one letter!
Isn't that grand?"*
—The White Queen to Alice in *Through the Looking Glass*

Ever since I wrote the very first edition of *One-Letter Words: A Dictionary,* I haven't had to pay for a single drink. But I didn't set out to create the ultimate secret weapon for winning bar bets. I mean, a dictionary is supposed to be scholarly, right? Then again, a dictionary like mine obviously doesn't belong sitting on a dusty reference shelf next to a highbrow encyclopedia. Something this weird was bound to grow wings of its own, and it has now found itself at the center of an Internet phenomenon, the recipient of a tribute song in Sweden, the subject of radio programs, and even a prop in stand-up comedy routines. Why? "Y" indeed!

Upon being told about my dictionary, the average person will laugh in disbelief, then—certain that I must be joking—ask just how many one-letter words there could possibly be. Nine out of ten people will guess that there are just two: the pronoun *I* and the article *a.* The occasional smarty-pants will grant that *O* might make a third, as in "O Romeo!" It's when I retort that there are 1,000 one-letter words that wagers get made—and won.

The fact of the matter is that a word is any letter or group of letters that has meaning and is used as a unit of language. So even though there are only twenty-six letters in the English alphabet, my research shows that they stand for 1,000 distinct units of meaning.

One-letter words are the building blocks of communication. I like to joke that learning them is easy and spelling them is even easier. But I definitely don't sell them short.

The most important English words are *small* ones. And those small words—which occur most often in our speech, reading, and writing—are relatively few in number. Just ten words account for 25 percent of all the words we use, and they all have only one syllable. Fifty words account for 50 percent of all the words in our speech, and they, too, all have only one syllable.

Two of the top six words we use in speech and writing have only one letter: *a* and *I*. *A* is the third most frequently occurring word in the English language. *I* is the sixth most frequently occurring. And there are other important one-letter words, which comprise the majority of my dictionary.

One of my favorites has to be *X*, which boasts more than seventy definitions of its own. X marks the spot on a pirate's map where treasure is buried. It's a hobo symbol meaning handouts are available. X tells you where to sign your name on a contract, and it's also an illiterate person's signature. X indicates a choice on a voting ballot and a cross-stitch of thread. Mysterious people may be named Madame X, and the archetype of a mad scientist is Dr. X. X is an incorrect answer on a test, and it's a rating for an adult movie. X is a power of magnification, an axis on a graph, and a female chromosome. It is a multiplication operator, a letter of the alphabet, and an arbitrary point in time. X is a kiss at the end of a love letter.

It's hard to pinpoint exactly when I first got the idea to write a dictionary of one-letter words. I remember once hearing about a bizarre Japanese crime novel from 1929, *The Devil's Apprentice* by Shiro Hamao, and how the entire work consisted of a single letter. The single letter was obviously a written correspondence, but I initially envisioned a single letter of the alphabet. And I marveled at how bizarre indeed it would be to write a detective story that all boiled down to a solitary letter of the alphabet. I imagined some sort of gritty retelling of Nathaniel Hawthorne's novel *The Scarlet Letter* in which a bloody letter *A* would serve as the only scrap of evidence to unravel a seedy tale of adultery, heartbreak, and murder.

I also remember how the poet Karen Drayne once wrote about an imaginary country where the language is so simple they have only one letter in the alphabet, and it works because "Context is everything." That got me thinking about how a single letter of the alphabet can represent all sorts of distinct meanings depending on the context.

I wrote the very first entry for my dictionary in a fit of procrastination. I was in graduate school, spending many hours a day in the library, purportedly working on my thesis. All those enormous unabridged dictionaries on the shelves intrigued me, and on a whim I started looking up the entries for the twenty-six letters of the alphabet. I jotted down all sorts of fascinating tidbits, and those notes became the bare bones for my dictionary of one-letter words. But I wasn't content to end it there. I knew that there must be even more meanings, and I went on a quest to discover them, scouring novels, plays, newspaper articles, magazine features, movie scripts, and writings on the Internet.

I wasn't satisfied with collecting mere definitions, however. I wanted to prove the legitimacy of those definitions with actual examples from literature. For example, one definition of *T* is "perfectly," and I found a simple quotation from the eighteenth-century novel *Tristram Shandy* to accompany it: "We could manage this matter to a T." For a rather boring definition of *W*, "someone designated W," I found a line by comedian Woody Allen: "Should I marry W? Not if she won't tell me the other letters in her name!"

The occasional idiosyncratic usage of a one-letter word didn't bother me, because I knew that people were discovering new concepts every day. Shakespeare, for example, coined more than 1,500 new words that were adopted into the popular culture. If people were using one-letter words in new ways, I wanted to be there to document them.

About four years ago, I finally put a free version of the book online at blueray.com, as a way of sharing my research with whatever audience I could find. I dedicated the Web version of my dictionary to the White Queen character from *Through the Looking Glass*. She famously told Alice, "I'll tell you a secret—I can read words of one letter! Isn't that grand?" It turned out that the White Queen and I weren't the only ones who were finding one-letter words to be grand.

All on its own, the online version of my dictionary was creating a firestorm of interest. In a matter of weeks, nearly 1,200 other Web sites were linking to my site. One hundred and forty of those sites were university, high school, and community libraries that recommend my dictionary on their reference links pages.

Bloggers were reviewing my work as well, giving it some funny praise. Doug MacClure called it "The most

perverse yet serious reference manual on the Web."
Edward Pelegrino called it "Interesting and possibly
useful." (I like his use of the word *possibly*. It's so full
of possibilities!) The Martinova blog dubbed it "Fun
for bored lit-geeks." I got the biggest kicks when I
found out the likes of professional wordsmith Richard
Lederer and Encyclopædia Britannica Online were
linking to my site. All this Web linkage reassured me
that while my research might be quirky it wasn't nec-
essarily superfluous.

Before I knew it, CNET Radio was e-mailing me to do
a spot on a morning program. I was initially terrified,
but I made it through an interview with talk show
host Alex Bennett in his "Weird Web Wednesday" seg-
ment.

Unbeknownst to me at the time, a musician in Sweden
was recording a tribute to my dictionary entitled, you
guessed it, "The Dictionary of One-Letter Words." Artist Kristofer Ström, whose band is called Ljudbilden
& Piloten, composed his ambient rock–style tribute
using guitar, bass, zither, trumpet, strings, drums,
human voice, and field recordings. Released by the
Barcelona label Nosordo Records in 2003, the track is
still receiving radio play.

As I read for pleasure, now and then I continue to find
new examples of usage to quote in my dictionary. So
the project is always growing and evolving. In addition to the free online version at blueray.com, a print
edition is available through CafePress.com.

I've lately branched out to write two smaller compan-
ion dictionaries: all-consonant words and all-vowel
words. These have been of particular interest to

Scrabble players, especially since I seek to document my definitions with literary citations. However, competitive Scrabble players have to be sticklers when it comes to rules, and I don't care to get in the middle of any controversy. I just do this stuff for fun.

To the best of my knowledge, my dictionary of one-letter words is the first-known such volume since the sixteenth century, when a Buddhist lexicographer named Saddhammakitti enumerated Pali words of one letter in a work entitled *Ekakkharakosa*. It may have taken 300 years to bridge the gap, but I like to think that Saddhammakitti's tradition lives on in my own dictionary of one-letter words.

AN ENTIRE ALPHABET OF
SCARLET LETTERS

I s it preposterous to wonder whether letters of the alphabet have an inherent color? As I conduct ongoing research for *One-Letter Words: A Dictionary*, I can't help but ask myself why it is that letters are so often described as having a rosy hue. Most readers will recall the infamous red *A* of Nathaniel Hawthorne's classic novel, but as Steven Heller pointed out, "*The Scarlet Letter* is not the only scarlet letter" (*The Education of an Illustrator*). Nor are scarlet letters solely brands of shame, sin, or doom. A "red-letter day" is a holiday, or at least a memorable or happy day (the phrase likely dating from 1549, when saint's days were marked in red in the *Book of Common Prayer*). Can there be a natural wavelength that writers instinctively pick up on? Virginia Woolf's eyes seemed keen enough to detect infrared all the way to *Z:* "After Q there are a number of letters the last of which is scarcely visible to mortal eyes, but glimmers red in the distance" (*To the Lighthouse*).

Biblical allusions associate the color scarlet with sins of the body, and by coloring their letters red, authors seem to flesh them out and add a spark of life. Take, for example, this description by Brian Moynahan: "[W]hen I came to read [the psalms], they seemed written in letters of fire or of scarlet" (*The Faith: A History of Christianity*). Nathaniel Hawthorne also mentioned a burning quality to his scarlet letter: "[Placing it to my breast,] I experienced a sensation not altogether physical, yet almost so, as of burning heat; and as if the letter were not of red cloth, but red-hot iron" (*The Scarlet Letter*). Sparkling red letters can even burn the imagination: "In my head a scarlet letter blazed," says Betty Fussell (*My Kitchen Wars*). Whether or not the context involves physical branding with a red-hot iron (examples would be rather too gruesome for inclusion here), blood imagery often figures in. As John Lawton wrote, "She rubbed the [handkerchief's embroidered] scarlet letter between finger and thumb, felt the crispness of dried blood" (*Bluffing Mr. Churchill*). George C. Chesbro dramatically combines blood and fire imagery in his depiction of an alphabet volcano "spewing what appeared to be incomplete, fractured sentences and clustered gobs of words that were half submerged in a river of blood red lava" (*The Language of Cannibals*). And consider this more serene example by poet Madeline Defrees, who seems to agree that scarlet letters are written by nature herself and in turn read by nature as well: "And who, /when scarlet letters/flutter in air from sumac and maple,/will be there to/receive them? Only a sigh/on the wind in the land of bending willow" ("Almanac," *Blue Dusk: New and Selected Poems, 1951–2001*).

In most cases, scarlet letters have a dazzling quality that you can't help but notice. Here's one example by Wilkie Collins: "[B]elow the small print appeared a perfect galaxy of fancifully shaped scarlet letters, which fascinated all eyes" (*Hide and Seek*). Groucho Marx recalled being fascinated by similar red letters: "In large, scarlet letters [the handbills] said, 'Would you like to communicate with your loved ones even though they are no longer in the flesh?' " (*Memoirs of a Mangy Lover*). It is as if the letters of Groucho's handbill had a rosy flesh of their own, and enough charge to bridge the gap between the living and the dead. Here's another example of a dazzling red letter from Ian Rankin: "There was a big letter X marking the spot [for a parachute jump]. It was made from two lengths of shiny red material, weighted down with stones" (*Resurrection Men: An Inspector Rebus Novel*).

Michael McCollum sums up nicely the impact of scarlet letters: "The [comet collision] display froze, save for a single blinking word etched in scarlet letters: *Impact!*" (*Thunderstrike!*) Red letters have impact, alright!

What follows is an entire alphabet of scarlet letters that I have collected, many as marks of shame but others simply pulsing with the red blush of life (or at least a strawberry birthmark). In a few cases I cite more than one favorite example from literature. Whether or not red is definitively the natural color of the alphabet is a question that is bound to remain controversial, but the body of evidence is certainly mounting.

A "The next day she had felt that the scarlet letter A—for Alcohol—was seared across her forehead, but her parents continued in their befuddled ignorance."—*This Body: A Novel of Reincarnation* by Laurel Doud

B "The shirt and bloomers [of the baseball suit] were gray, with narrow red stripes. There were two big red letter B's lying loose in the box." —*Carney's House Party* by Maud Hart Lovelace

C "From now on Joe is the man with the Scarlet Letter. He has 'C' [for Communist] written on his coat, put there by men who know him best."— *Joseph McCarthy: Reexamining the Life and Legacy of America's Most Hated Senator* by Arthur Herman

D "Some of the women students dressed in black and pinned a red 'D' on their sweaters. 'It's my scarlet letter,' one explained. 'I dance. I'm a sinner.' "—*Lost Revolutions: The South in the 1950s* by Pete Daniel

"[S]ince there is a no-fault divorce law, a party can be perfectly innocent and still get the scarlet letter—in this case a D—stitched on his shirt."—*Breach of Promise* by James Scott Bell

E "Barring sewing a scarlet letter E on her clothes, they knew enough about her daughter's mental illness [erotomania] and past history to keep her away from, or at least warn, any female authority figures who might unwittingly cross her path."—*I Know You Really Love Me: A Psychiatrist's Account of Stalking and Obsessive Love* by Doreen Orion

F "[T]here had been an incomplete letter painted in blood red on Sarah's wall. At the time, Francesca and Bragg had thought it might be an F." —*Deadly Caress* by Brenda Joyce

"I was going to fail. Fail! No B, no gentleman's C—Fail. F. The big one: my own Scarlet Letter. Branded on my forehead—F, for Fuckup."—*A Fistful of Fig Newtons* by Jean Shepherd

"Never mind that they are doctors, lawyers, world leaders; they must still wear a scarlet letter, a giant red F, if, heaven forbid, they're fat."—*The Blessed* by Sharon McMahon Moffitt

G "The first illustration was of a young man with short wavy hair and a fringe of reddish beard, standing by himself inside the arc of a giant red G." —*Codex* by Lev Grossman

H "You look and smell like a street whore from the slums. Did you know it is within regulations for me to brand you with the letter H for harlot? . . . Tomorrow night I will fetch the brand which imprints the scarlet letter. I think I will put it upon your breasts. Yes, an H upon each. Two H's.

They will brand you forever as Helford's Harlot!"
—*The Pirate and the Pagan* by Virginia Henley

I   "Has a big red letter 'I' appeared on my chest,
branding me as infertile to the world?"—"The
Goddess Speaks" by Dot Shigemura

J   "If they do walk free, they should carry a warning to the rest of us. Maybe a scarlet letter J, for
jackal, sewn onto all their clothes."—"Bottom
Line Attracts Bottom Feeders" by Michael Miller

"Unless Jesus appears before us with a scarlet
letter J on His forehead and unless Jesus shows
us the wounds in His side we treat Him as just
another of life's encounters or acquaintances."
—"Prayers of the Passion" by Sue Eidahl

K   "Mark born or unborn [children] with a red letter
K."—"Count Your Sins" by Audrey Tarvids

L   "It was like I'd been branded with a scarlet let-
ter L for liar, and I felt as though no one treated
me the same for weeks after that."—*Emotional
Blackmail: When the People in Your Life Use Fear,
Obligation, and Guilt to Manipulate You* by Susan
Forward

"For years, many on the left have ducked the 'L'
word. While characterized by the right as pink,
the letter, unfortunately, has become tainted as
scarlet."—*Red, White & Liberal: How Left Is Right
& Right Is Wrong* by Alan Colmes

M   "Sometimes, I feel as though I'm wearing a hor-
rifying scarlet letter—only the letter is M, for
Murderess."—*Hide and Seek* by James Patterson

"Even when out on her own she felt as if she were wearing a scarlet letter. M for miscegenist."
—*Cloud Mountain* by Aimee Liu

N "When a brand-new exhibitor with her first dog joins a kennel club, she wears a large scarlet letter (N for Novice) on her breast that is visible to everyone but her."—*Dog Showing for Beginners* by Lynn Hall

O "A giant O [referring to the stigma of an open relationship] would hang above our house, a scarlet letter emblazoned upon the sky for the general protection of the citizenry."—*The Bastard on the Couch: 27 Men Try Really Hard to Explain Their Feelings About Love, Loss, Fatherhood, and Freedom* by Daniel Jones

P "Halfway up the hill a prominent lump of gray stone the size of a hayrick had been painted with a large, lop-sided letter P in scarlet paint, so that it was visible to any ship anchored in the lagoon."—*Blue Horizon* by Wilbur Smith

Q "I didn't know that there was a pain like that in the world. And I writhed from the torture of it—a clotted red letter 'Q' spread across my eyes and started to quiver."—*Die Reise nach Petuschki* by Wenedikt Jerofejew

R "Our lucite deal mementos would need to be amended to add this [subscript] R, now the scarlet letter of derivatives."—*F.I.A.S.C.O.: The Inside Story of a Wall Street Trader* by Frank Partnoy

"The weight of an invisible scarlet letter R, for rapist."—*The Pledge* by Rob Kean

S "Once she was defeated, she put on the scarlet letter—S for secrecy and shame—and did not tell either of her two husbands or her son about me."—*Journey of the Adopted Self: A Quest for Wholeness* by Betty Jean Lifton

" 'It's all getting to be a real burden for those of us who still smoke.' Susan Saunders says. 'Today's "scarlet letter" is the big red S we smokers feel we wear around our necks.' "—*The No-Nag, No-Guilt, Do-It-Your-Own Way Guide to Quitting Smoking* by Tom Ferguson

T "I was only good for punishment, and punished I was, never fear. I pinned on my scarlet letter—mine would be a T, for toe-sucking—and wore it everywhere, with a sort of perverse comfort."—*My Story* by Sarah Ferguson

"Basically, being temporary means you don't exist in the federal system. You're invisible.... Do I get to have a scarlet letter T painted on my forehead?"—*The Loop: A Novel* by Nicholas Evans

U "[A]nyone who challenges their policies is threatened with the new Scarlet Letter—U—for Unpatriotic."—"Support Our Troops?" by Gregory Reck

V "Although self-pity thwarts self-acceptance, wearing the scarlet letter V (for victim) allows us to take the moral high ground."—*Ruthless Trust: The Ragamuffin's Path to God* by Brennan Manning

"[W]hat have we come to, that the scarlet letter these days isn't A, but V [for Virginity]?"—*Him/Her/Self: Gender Identities in Modern America* by Peter G. Filene

W "Davenport marked all nomads in his [eugenics] table with a scarlet W (for Wanderlust, the common German term for 'urge to roam'). He then examined the distribution of W's through families and generations to reach one of the most peculiar and improbable of conclusions ever advanced in a famous study: nomadism, he argued, is caused by a single gene."—*The Lying Stones of Marrakech: Penultimate Reflections in Natural History* by Stephen Jay Gould

X "Branded with the scarlet letter 'X' in the new MPAA ratings system, *Midnight Cowboy* nonetheless encountered absolutely no difficulties at the box office."—*The Sixties: 1960–1969* by Paul Monaco

Y "[I]t is the symbols of Communism that return to attack and kill Benny, and in the last lines of [Benedikt Erofeev's] novel [*Moscow Circles*], it is the red letter 'Y' that spreads before Benny's eyes as he dies. Throughout the novel, it is this letter that has symbolized Benny's participation in the symbolic order, as it is the only letter his baby son knows."—"Moscow Circles" by Avril Tonkin

Z "Sesar got up and looked at his watch. In the center of the black face was a red letter Z. It began to flash."—*Neo-Zed* by Anonymous

THE LETTERS OF THE ALPHABET AS OUR ROAD MAP TO THE MINDSCAPE

The Croatian-American writer Josip Nova-kovich made a fascinating observation about learning a second language. Cut off from the umbilical of his mother tongue, he found the freedom to experiment. As he puzzled out how to spell a new word, or rearranged phrases and sentences, pictures began forming in his mind, and those pictures opened doors into "imagined countries, histories, songs, and silences." He likened it to playing with those colorful letter building blocks from childhood, and he took great pleasure in constructing the contours of his own imaginary spaces. "[W]riting in English became a way to carve out a place for myself," he said. "It was what allowed me to negotiate a space in which I had control over events and landscapes, to shape the world according to private experience" (*Stories in the Stepmother Tongue*).

What an intriguing concept—individual letters of the alphabet shaping the topography of a mental landscape that had been there all along, marking out the spots of buried treasures you didn't know you had.

Author Dana Redfield had an experience similar to Novakovich's when she began looking at her native English alphabet from a different perspective. Her study of the geometry of the letterforms "spilled so much light into my mind, it seemed to brighten out a mystical landscape beyond the borders of my normal consciousness" (*The ET-Human Link*). It was as if the closer she looked at the alphabet letters, the more she could detect the architectural forms of a previously hidden world. Of course, scholars of the sacred Hebrew and Sanskrit letterforms (to name but two ancient scripts) have for centuries been making similar claims that an alphabet can illuminate other worlds.

What fun it is to allow letters to reveal landscapes of the mind, and to trace out the shapes of letters in the natural world. Albert Einstein once said of Isaac Newton, "Nature was to him an open book, whose letters he could read without effort." This flies in the face of Sigmund Freud, however, who wrote in *The Interpretation of Dreams* that letters of the alphabet have no right in a landscape, "since such objects do not occur in nature." Could Freud have been wrong? After all, painters often seem to read the letters in nature, evident in how they work alphabet shapes into their compositions to lead the viewer's eye toward a focal point. "For instance," says art expert Mary Whyte, "the letters C, L, Z, J, V, or S can be seen underlying many compositions," whether consciously depicted or not (*Watercolor for the Serious Beginner*). And nature photographer Kjell B. Sandved found the entire alphabet depicted on the wings of moths and butterflies—even if it did take him more than twenty-five years and visits to more than thirty countries to discover every letter. He concluded that "Nature's message is clear for all to see . . . it is written on the wings of butterflies!" (*The Butterfly Alphabet*).

Individual letters are the smallest elements of words, and words are the smallest elements of thought. It's no wonder, then, that when people try to imagine what the creative process might *look* like, they often picture *letters of the alphabet* swirling around in someone's head.

At Walt Disney World's Epcot theme park, the original Journey into Imagination pavilion took guests into a three-dimensional mock-up of the brain's storehouse of information. At one point during the ride, visitors saw a character named Dreamfinder seated at the console of a giant typewriter, the top of which was a trembling volcano. As Dreamfinder touched the keys, letters exploded out of the volcano and drifted down as words, falling onto the pages of a book.

Such a mental landscape—or "mindscape"—sought to turn an abstract concept ("thought," "imagination," "creativity") into a concrete one. A mindscape offers us a common point of reference when we venture into the mysterious world of the mind. Authors present mindscapes to their readers all the time. They do it so that we can understand what makes a character tick.

In the following passage from the novel *The Arabian Nightmare,* author Robert Irwin imagines what it's like in the deepest part of the mind, the part that we have inherited from, our most distant ancestors and that links us to them.

> [One] became aware, albeit always dimly, of something small at the centre of the brain beyond reach of thought or memory, quite beyond conscious seizing—the primal matter of consciousness perhaps. One glimpsed from a great distance an area, brilliantly lit by internal flashes of lightning, in which tiny little men flickered and ran carrying letters, emblems and numbers amid blocks of flashing rods and colours. It was beyond meaning.

This deepest part of the mind exists far beneath the thinking part of our brain, beyond words and concepts. It is aptly described as a turbulent world of flashing lights and colors, where little people run around transporting individual letters, numbers, and other symbols—the building blocks of consciousness.

The following quotation from Milorad Pavic's novel *Dictionary of the Khazars* has some marked similarities to the previous passage:

> The Khazars saw letters in people's dreams,
> and in them they looked for primordial man,
> for Adam Cadmon. . . . They believed that
> to every person belongs one letter of the
> alphabet, that each of these letters constitutes
> part of Adam Cadmon's body on earth, and
> that these letters converge in people's dreams
> and come to life in Adam's body.

Here, too, the author believes part of our brain links us to our ancient ancestors. In this case, it goes all the way back to Adam, the archetype of the first human. Letters of the alphabet appear in this passage, also. They are the stuff that dreams are made of. They also symbolize the very building blocks of our existence.

Science fiction authors like Pat Cadigan (*Mindplayers*) and Greg Bear foresee the day when scientists will be able to enter into a person's mindscape via high-tech tools. In Bear's novel *Queen of Angels*, psychologists step into the mind of a murderer and find a mental city on whose sidewalks misshapen letters are scribbled and on whose walls posters of "everchanging, meaningless letters" are plastered.

Until the future that Bear describes arrives, we must be content to *imagine* the hills and valleys that make up the landscape of the mind. But we aren't without a guide. The letters of the alphabet are our passport and our road map. The authors quoted above seem to suggest that the alphabet spells out the answers to all of life's questions. We must simply find the right combinations.

ONE-LETTER
WORDS
a Dictionary

A IN PRINT AND PROVERB

1. (phrase) *A per se* means "*a* by itself makes the word *a*."

2. (phrase) *Not to know A from B* means to be ignorant.
   "How are your brains?"
   "I know A from B and two plus two," I answered him.
   "That'll do. The rest you can learn." —Karen Cushman, *Matilda Bone*

3. (phrase) *Not to know A from a windmill*, a popular expression until the nineteenth century, means to be ignorant.
   [Mid-fifteenth-century poet Frian Daw Topias's] characterization of himself as ... not knowing an "a" from a windmill or a "b" from a bull's foot seems to go beyond the conventional modesty topos of other writers. —James Dean, *Six Ecclesiastical Satires*

4. (in literature) *A, black hairy corset of dazzling flies/Who boom around cruel stenches,/Gulfs of darkness* —Arthur Rimbaud, "Vowels"

5. (in literature) Nathaniel Hawthorne's *Scarlet Letter* concerns a woman condemned to wear an *A* (for the crime of adultery) embroidered on her breast. Any woman wearing such a letter was shunned by society. Here's what Hawthorne writes in the first chapter: "On the breast of her gown, in red cloth, surrounded with elaborate embroidery and fantastic flourishes of gold thread, appeared the letter *A*." The description makes it seem beautiful—doesn't that make the symbolic meaning all the more serious and chilling?
   After all, A is really harmless enough, even if A is the scarlet letter. —William H. Gass, *The Tunnel*

6. (in literature) *"Do you know what A means, little Piglet? . . . It means Learning, it means Education, it means all the things that you and Pooh haven't got."* —A. A. Milne, *The World of Pooh*

7. (in literature) *"A is the roof, the gable with its crossbeam, the arch; or it is two friends greeting, who embrace and shake hands."* —Victor Hugo, quoted in *ABZ* by Mel Gooding

8. (in film) The title of a ten-minute short film from Germany, written and directed by Jan Lenica in 1965. The synopsis states: "A writer is persecuted by an enormous and abusive letter 'A.' Just as he thinks he has gotten rid of it, a giant 'B' appears."

9. *n.* A written representation of the letter. *[3-D graphic designer Peter Cho] points to a dancing A and challenges me to define the properties of this or any other letter. Cutting-edge technology allows us to give letters virtually any form, he says, but the brain somehow provides the mental ability to recognise a specific letter.* —Leo Gullbring, "The Rebirth of Space" in *Frame Magazine*

10. *n.* A device, such as a printer's type, for reproducing the letter.

POINTS IN TIME AND SPACE

11. *n.* The beginning, as in "from A to Z." *Intuition is the journey from A to Z without stopping at any other letter along the way.* —Gavin De Becker, *The Gift of Fear: Survival Signals That Protect Us from Violence*

12. *n.* The first letter of the alphabet.
    *Her embarcation card, filed under A, had eluded
    the search made by the harbour police.* —Georges
    Perec, *Life: A User's Manual*
    *A is the inside, as it were, the origin and source
    from which the other letters flow, and likewise the
    final goal to which all the others flow back, as
    rivers flow into the ocean or into the great sea.*
    —Hermes, "Tractatus aureus" (Golden Treatise
    of Hermes)

13. *prep.* In each.
    *[E]ach dialysis session bothered him less, and by
    now he was used to being hooked to the machine
    three times* a *week.* —Sanjay Nigam, *Transplanted
    Man: A Novel*

14. *prep.* (informal) Of. *Have you the time* a *day?*

15. *n.* A precursor.
    *[A] feeling of timelessness, the feeling that what we
    know as time is only the result of a naïve faith in
    causality—the notion that A in the past caused B in
    the present, which will cause C in the future.* —Tom
    Wolfe, *The Electric Kool-Aid Acid Test*

16. *n.* A high-level perception of cosmic unity, beyond
    causality.
    *[A]ctually A, B, and C are all part of a pattern
    that can be truly understood only by opening the
    doors of perception and experiencing it . . . in this
    moment . . . this supreme moment . . . this* kairos.
    —Tom Wolfe, *The Electric Kool-Aid Acid Test*

17. *n.* Waking consciousness.
    *Allegorically, the initial A of [the sacred Hindu syl-
    lable] AUM is said to represent the field and state of
    Waking Consciousness, where objects are of "gross*

*matter"... and are separate both from each other
and from the consciousness beholding them.*
—Joseph Campbell, *The Mythic Image*

MUSIC

18. *n.* The sixth note in a C-major musical scale.
    *Suppose you played the note A on a piano, and then
    went up eight white keys to another A. A musician
    would say the second A is one "octave" higher than
    the first A.* —David M. Schwartz, *Q Is for Quark: A
    Science Alphabet Book*

19. *n.* A written or printed representation of a musical
    note A.

20. *n.* A string, key, or pipe tuned to the note A.

21. *n.* The first section in a piece of music.
    *The final passacaglia's five bar theme is clearly
    derived from section A of the Chorale and its sur-
    prising five bar phrasing.* —OrganConcert.info

DESIGNATIONS

22. *n.* A standard, as in "A one."
    Her gears being in/A 1 shape. —e. e. Cummings,
    "she being Brand"

23. *n.* A grade in school meaning superior.
    *The second skit [starring comedian Paul Lynde as
    an aging criminal who is heartbroken to learn his
    son is growing into a law-abiding honor student]
    included the funniest use of a single letter in film
    history: Lynde clutches his son's report card and,
    horrified at the academic excellence which will*

ultimately deny him an heir in his crime business, runs off-screen screaming aloud the boy's straight A grades, stretching the letter "A" into a piercing wail of Greek tragedy proportions. —Phil Hall, in a *Film Threat* review of the 1954 musical comedy *New Faces*

24. *n.* One graded with an A.
My husband gives me an A/for last night's supper, /an incomplete for my ironing. —Linda Pastan, "Marks"

25. *n.* Something arbitrarily designated A (e.g., a person, place, or other thing).
Historical attention is like needle and thread going in and out of the holes of a button, fastening A to B only by passing through both many times. —William H. Gass, *The Tunnel*

26. *article.* A particular one. *men all of a sort*

27. *prep.* Per. *Eggs are 60¢ a dozen.*

28. *prep.* Any single. *Not a one made it through alive.*

29. *prep.* Any certain one. *A Mr. Po called.*

30. *prep.* Another. *a Mona Lisa in beauty*

SHAPES AND SIZES

31. *n.* Something having the shape of an A.

32. *n.* A-frame: a triangular supporting frame; a triangular, all-roof building.
A-frame enthusiasts in the 1950s and 1960s were correct in asserting that the form had an ancient lineage. The simplicity, strength, and versatility of . . . triangu-

lar structures explain why they were so common for so many centuries. —Chad Randl, *A-Frame*

33. *n.* A shoe width size (wider than AA, narrower than B).

34. *n.* A brassiere cup size.
    Bust circumference is determined by measuring the circumference of the chest loosely with a tape around the fullest part of the breasts, usually at the level of the nipples, with the woman ordinarily wearing a bra. Cup size is then determined by comparing the bust circumference to the underbust plus five measurement. A difference of 1 inch equals an A cup, 2 inches a B cup, 3 inches a C cup, and so on. For example, a woman with a bust circumference of 36 inches and a band size of 34 (underbust chest circumference or 29 + 5 inches) would be a B cup (36 - 34 = 2 inch difference = B cup). —Edward A. Pechter, M.D., *Breast Measurement*

35. *n.* A-shirt: a T-shirt without sleeves.

MISCELLANEOUS

36. *n.* The lightest weight of sandpaper available.
    The letter A signifies the lightest weight of paper used. —Bruce E. Johnson, *The Wood Finisher*

37. *n.* Any spoken sound represented by the letter.
    The sound vibration of the vowel A means "washing, purity, purification, purifying light." —Joseph E. Rael, *Tracks of Dancing Light: A Native American Approach to Understanding Your Name*

38. *v.* (chiefly informal) Have. *He'd a done it if he wanted to.*

39. *v.* (slang) Going to.
   I'm a do it like this. —The Rap Dictionary

SCIENTIFIC MATTERS

40. *n.* A vitamin (retinol/carotene).
   *Vitamin A is particularly associated with eye
   health, because it protects the surface of the cor-
   nea. It is also essential for the development of bones,
   growth, and reproduction. It helps the body resist
   infection by protecting the linings of the respira-
   tory, digestive, and urinary tracts and maintains
   healthy skin and hair. Beta carotene (also known
   as pro vitamin A) is converted to vitamin A by the
   body. Unlike retinol, beta carotene is an antioxi-
   dant—a substance that protects the body against
   disease and premature aging by fighting the cell-
   damaging chemicals called free radicals.... Good
   sources of vitamin A are liver and fish-liver oils,
   egg yolk, milk and dairy products, and margarine.
   Beta carotene is found in dark-green and deep-
   yellow fruits and vegetables, such as carrots, apri-
   cots, and spinach.* —American Medical Association

41. *n.* A blood type.
   *Genes for types A and B are dominant, and will
   always be expressed. Type O is recessive. A child
   who inherits one A and one O gene will be type A.
   Similarly, a child who inherits one B and one O gene
   will be type B. If both an A and a B gene are passed
   on, a child will be type AB. Only a child who inherits
   one O gene from each parent will be type O.*
   —Mayo Clinic

42. *n.* A person with type A blood.
   If you are Type A ... and the meat you keep eating is

9

not metabolizing, your bloodstream is now flooded with thick, sticky agglutinated blood, loaded with saturated animal fat, just looking for a nice spot to deposit itself. It doesn't take a genius IQ to see why A's ... should not eat meat, and if they do, they die younger. —Steven M. Weissberg, MD, *InnerSelf Magazine*

43. *n.* A level: an ancient Egyptian level shaped like the letter A: "The crossbar has a line marking its center. A string is attached to the top of the A, and a weight keeps it taut. When the string hangs down right by the crossbar marking, the crossbar is level." —Dr. John Burkardt

44. *n.* (biology) Adenine, one of the four nitrogenous bases found in DNA nucleotides.

45. *n.* (electronics) A battery: "A supply."

46. *n.* (logic) The notation of a universal affirmative statement, such as "all humans are mammals." In categorical logic, the square of opposition describes the relationship between the universal affirmative *A*, the universal negative *E*, the particular affirmative *I*, and the particular negative *O*.

47. *n.* (mathematics) A matrix.
The use of a single letter A to represent a matrix was crucial to the development of matrix algebra. —Marie A. Vitulli, "A Brief History of Linear Algebra and Matrix Theory"

48. *n.* (astronomy) A class of white stars.
When an astronomer speaks of a class A star, he refers to white stars like Sirius and Vega, in whose spectra we see a very strong series of dark lines caused by hydrogen in the atmosphere. —Dennis Richard Danielson, *The Book of the Cosmos*

49. *n.* A horizon: the dark-colored layer of topsoil, made up of humus and mineral particles, where seeds germinate.

FOREIGN MEANINGS

50. *n.* (Spanish) Point, as in *a por a y be por be,* "point by point."

FACTS AND FIGURES

51. Vowel symbols were invented 5,000 years ago by the Sumerians (an ancient people of Mesopotamia). Their cuneiform writing was made up of pictures that represented syllables, but they had special characters for the vowels *A, E, I,* and *U.* But *A* traces its origins back to ancient Egypt, where it was symbolized by a picture of an eagle. Yet *A* started out as a consonant! Egyptian hieroglyphics did not have vowels—the eagle simply represented the *A* sound.

52. One-letter words like "A" require a context in order to communicate meaning.
    We must remember that for something to be information, there is a requirement: If the set of parts is quite short, it lacks complexity to be sure that it constitutes information. For example, if we had a one-letter word, then there could easily be a very good chance that the word may have arisen from a random choice of letters. In such an instance, we could not make a good case for proving that the small word is actually information that came from an intelligent source—because there is not enough complexity. Secondly, the length of the string of letters must be of sufficient length to perform the

function of communication. For example, the letter "A" is a word, but without being part of a phrase or sentence, we have no assurance that it actually functions to communicate anything. —R. Totten, A Mathematical Proof of Intelligent Design in Nature

B IN PRINT AND PROVERB

1. **(phrase)** *Not to know B from a bull's foot* means to be illiterate.
   In 1916, Atlanta mayor James G. Woodward, a union printer at the Atlanta Journal, *lampooned the pretentiousness of the city's grand opera patrons, declaring that Atlantans "don't know B from bull's foot about grand opera, although they go and make a lot of fuss about it."* —Cliff Kuhn, *Contesting the New South Order: The 1914–1915 Strike at Atlanta's Fulton Mills*

2. **(in film)** The title of a ten-minute Spanish short film written and directed by Daniel Vázquez Salles.

3. **(in literature)** Said of someone's face: *"Fair as a text B in a copy-book."* —William Shakespeare, *Love's Labor's Lost*, V.ii.42

4. **(in literature)** *"B is the back on the back, the hump."* —Victor Hugo, quoted in *ABZ* by Mel Gooding

5. **(in literature)** *"B is parkgate."* —James Joyce, *Ulysses*

6. *n.* A written representation of the letter.
   The villainous girlfriend turned all the way around to show off her [snowsuit] outfit from every angle. Sunny looked up from her cooking and noticed that the letter B was sewn onto the back of it, along with the eye insignia. —Lemony Snicket, *The Slippery Slope* (A Series of Unfortunate Events, Book 10)

7. *n.* A device, such as a printer's type, for reproducing the letter.

8. *n.* A book.
   Speaking of the B-word—in my relaxed, between-job languor I actually read one. —Christine Borne, "Nextgen Librarian"

SECONDS, ANYONE?

9. *n.* The second in a series.

10. *n.* The second letter of the alphabet.
    Reference to the biographies . . . of all women singers whose name began with B. —Georges Perec, *Life: A User's Manual*

11. *n.* A grade in school indicating "better than average."

12. *n.* One graded with a B.
    [U]ndue reliance upon grades or law school pedigree may be misguided—in the words of the familiar law school maxim, "The A students make professors, the B students make judges, and the C students make money." —Ellen Weisbord, *Managing People in Today's Law Firm: The Human Resources Approach to Surviving Change*

13. *adj.* Secondary, inferior.

MUSIC AND MUSICIANS

14. (phrase) *The Three B's:* Bach, Beethoven, and Brahms.
    [Sir Thomas] Beecham generally tried his best to avoid the three B's: Bach, Beethoven, and Brahms. In fact he was known to feign sickness before performances of Beethoven's Ninth Symphony.
    —Steven Staryk, *Fiddling with Life: The Unusual Journey of Steven Staryk*

B

15. *n.* The seventh note in a C-major musical scale.

16. *n.* A written or printed representation of a musical note B.

17. *n.* A string, key, or pipe tuned to the note B.

18. *n.* The second section in a piece of music.

SHAPES AND SIZES

19. *n.* A large size of shot.

20. *n.* Something having the shape of a B.
    The important thing is that there must be no
    restriction in the throat and that the lips must
    remain in the "B" shape as the air is expelled.
    —Larry Hudson, *Bandworld Magazine*
    The squat shirt-sleeved Jew whose tight belt cut
    his round belly into the letter B turned to the lime-
    streaked wop—squinted, saw that communication
    had failed. —Henry Roth, *Call It Sleep*

21. *n.* A shoe width size (wider than A, narrower than C).
    Most men's shoes are in a D width and women's in a B
    width. —Joe Ellis, *Running Injury-Free: How to Prevent,*
    Treat, and Recover from Dozens of Painful Problems

22. *n.* A brassiere cup size.
    I didn't belong around no hungry babies because
    I'd squeezed inside a B-cup bra so there was three
    inches of cleavage spilling over. —Yxta Maya
    Murray, *What It Takes to Get to Vegas*

B

MISCELLANEOUS

23. *n.* Any spoken sound represented by the letter.
    *The sound vibration of the consonant B means
    "straight, sacred path."* —Joseph E. Rael, *Tracks
    of Dancing Light: A Native American Approach to
    Understanding Your Name*
    *Her eyes were puffy. Her words were full of the
    sound of the letter b. She watched Clarence while
    holding tissues to her nose.* —Tracy Kidder, *Among
    Schoolchildren*

24. *n.* (slang) A word used to address a friend.
    Yo, chill b. —*The Rap Dictionary*

25. *n.* A Roman numeral for 300.

26. *n.* Something arbitrarily designated B (e.g., a per-
    son, place, or other thing).
    B said that A is the spy. —Raymond Smullyan, *The
    Lady or the Tiger?*

27. *adj.* A mediocre movie, usually low-budget.
    *I learned the delirious pleasure of watching old "B"
    movies in the dead of night.* —Eddie Muller, *Dark
    City: The Lost World of Film Noir*
    *The film was among the first musical productions
    shot in CinemaScope and director Harry Horner, a
    B-movie helmer who rose to create his only A-level
    production here, wonderfully fills the extra-wide
    screen during the kinetic dance interludes.* —Phil
    Hall, in a *Film Threat* review of the 1954 musical
    comedy *New Faces*

SCIENTIFIC MATTERS

28. *n.* A class of vitamins including B1 (thiamine), B2
    (riboflavin), B3 (niacin), B5 (pantothenic acid), B6
    (pyridoxine), and B12 (cyanocobalamin).

Vitamin B12 works with folic acid to build the genetic material of cells and produce blood cells in bone marrow. It is also involved in the activities of some of the body's enzymes (substances that promote chemical reactions in the body) and helps maintain a healthy nervous system. . . . The best sources of vitamin B12 are organ meats. Fish (especially sardines, herring, and oysters), lean meats, poultry, cheese, and eggs are also good sources. The only known plant sources are yeast, alfalfa, and two Japanese seaweeds—wakame and kombu. —American Medical Association

29. *n.* A blood type.
    Genes for types A and B are dominant, and will always be expressed. Type O is recessive. A child who inherits one A and one O gene will be type A. Similarly, a child who inherits one B and one O gene will be type B. If both an A and a B gene are passed on, a child will be type AB. Only a child who inherits one O gene from each parent will be type O. —Mayo Clinic

30. *n.* A person with type B blood.

31. *n.* (electronics) Susceptance.

32. *n.* (electronics) A battery, as in "B supply."

33. *n.* (chemistry) The symbol for the element boron in the periodic table.

34. *n.* An event in the present caused by something in the past.
    [A] feeling of timelessness, the feeling that what we know as time is only the result of a naïve faith in causality—the notion that A in the past caused B in the present, which will cause C in the future. —Tom Wolfe, *The Electric Kool-Aid Acid Test*

35. *n.* A high-level perception of cosmic unity, beyond causality.
[A]ctually, A, B, and C are all part of a pattern that can be truly understood only by opening the doors of perception and experiencing it . . . in this moment . . . this supreme moment . . . this kairos.
—Tom Wolfe, *The Electric Kool-Aid Acid Test*

36. *n.* (astronomy) A class of blue-white stars.
For blue-white stars like Rigel we use the letter B. — Dennis Richard Danielson, *The Book of the Cosmos*

37. *n.* B horizon: the layer of subsoil accumulating deposits from mineralized water in the soil above.

FOREIGN MEANINGS

38. *n.* (French) *Être marqué au b* means to be one-eyed or hump-backed. Set in the Middle Ages, *The Hunchback of Notre Dame* tells the story of Quasimodo, a grotesquely deformed bell ringer at the Notre Dame Cathedral in Paris. The French might have said of Quasimodo: *Il est marqué au b.* "He is hump-backed."

39. *n.* (Hebrew) The letter *B* is called *beth,* which means "a house."

FACTS AND FIGURES

40. In the Middle Ages, a *B* was branded on a blasphemer's forehead.

B

C IN PRINT AND PROVERB

1. (in literature) Said of handwriting: *"By my life, this is my lady's hand. These be her very c's, her u's, and her t's, and thus she makes she her great P's."* —William Shakespeare, *Twelfth Night,* II.v.86–88 (The speaker here has unwittingly spelled out the word *cut,* slang for the female pudenda. The joke is carried further by "her *great P's.*")

2. (in literature) *"C is where murder took place."* —James Joyce, *Ulysses*

3. (in literature) Described as an infuriating letter: *"[Volume 3 of* The Oxford English Dictionary,*] embracing the entirety of the infuriating letter C (which the lexicographers found unusually filled with ambiguities and complexities, not least because of its frequent overlaps with the letters G, K, and S)—should be dedicated to [Queen Victoria in 1896]."* —Simon Winchester, *The Professor and the Madman: A Tale of Murder, Insanity, and the Making of "The Oxford English Dictionary"*

4. (in literature) *"C is the crescent, the moon."* —Victor Hugo, quoted in *ABZ* by Mel Gooding

5. *n.* A written representation of the letter. *On his arm, she saw the tattoo, a blue letter C.* —Philip K. Dick, *The Man in the High Castle*

6. *n.* A device, such as a printer's type, for reproducing the letter.

GENEROUS AMOUNTS

7. *n.* A Roman numeral for 100. *[T]he first letter of his name was struck from the inscription on his [Augustus's] statue by a bolt of*

*lightning. This was understood to mean that he
would only live for a further hundred days, for
that was the significance of the letter "C," and that
it would come to pass that he would be included
among the gods, for "aesar," the remaining part of
the name "Caesar," means "god" in the language of
the Etruscans.* —Suetonius, *Lives of the Caesars*

8. *n.* With a line over it, a Roman numeral for 100,000.

9. *n.* (slang) A one-hundred-dollar bill, as in "C-note."
    *When a starlet or a pretty showgirl sat beside
    Costello, there would be a C-note staring at her
    when the waiter removed her plate.* —Evan
    Thomas, *The Man to See*

10. *n.* A shoe width size (wider than B, narrower than D).

11. *n.* A brassiere cup size.
    *The first contraceptive pill released in 1960 had
    ten times as much [estrogen] as versions that came
    along later. The sale of C-cup bras increased 50
    percent during the sixties, as all that estrogen
    caused women's breasts to swell.* —Gail Collins,
    *America's Women: Four Hundred Years of Dolls,
    Drudges, Helpmates, and Heroines*

THE KEY OF C

12. *n.* C clef: a symbol placed upon a staff to indicate
    the location of middle C.

13. *n.* The first note in a C-major musical scale.
    *You can think of [the note C in a C scale] as "home."
    Most songs will go on a journey, but they will
    always want to come back to their home eventually.*

—E. D. Hirsch, *What Your Fourth Grader Needs to Know: Fundamentals of a Good Fourth-Grade Education (The Core Knowledge)*

14. *n.* A written or printed representation of a musical note C.

15. *n.* A string, key, or pipe tuned to the note C.

16. *n.* The third section in a piece of music.

17. *n.* C hole: a C-shaped sound hole in a guitar or viol.

IN THIRD PLACE

18. *n.* Something arbitrarily designated C (e.g., a person, place, or other thing).

19. *n.* Someone called C.
    Mr. C glad-handed the boss-men of the ship-breaking concern that would be scrapping the vessel.
    —Iain Banks, *The Business*
    After dinner it was agreed that we should walk, when I had finished a letter to C, part of which I had written in the morning by the kitchen-fire while the mutton was roasting. —Dorothy Wordsworth, *The Grasmere and Alfoxden Journals*

20. *n.* A grade in school indicating "average."

21. *n.* One graded with a C.
    A Yale University president some years ago gave this advice to a former president of Ohio State: "Always be kind to your A and B students. Someday one of them will return to your campus as a good professor. And also be kind to your C students.

Someday one of them will return and build a two-million-dollar science laboratory." —John C. Maxwell, *The Winning Attitude*

22. *n.* The third in a series.

MISCELLANEOUS

23. *n.* The third letter of the alphabet.
Neither the letter C, they say, nor the letter K had ever harmed the city. —Julian, *Misopogon*

24. *n.* Any spoken sound represented by the letter.
The sound vibration of the consonant C means "beauty, beautify." —Joseph E. Rael, *Tracks of Dancing Light: A Native American Approach to Understanding Your Name*

25. *n.* C-rations: food provided to soldiers during combat.
C-rations were two cans, smaller than a normal soup can. One held crackers, soluble coffee or tea, lemonade, bouillon, sugar, toilet paper, candy and four cigarettes. The other can held food to be warmed. Beef stew, chicken and noodles, Spam and potatoes, corned beef hash, etc. —John C. McManus, *The Deadly Brotherhood*

SHAPES AND SIZES

26. *n.* Something having the shape of a C.
She had this very distinctive shape, seemingly comprised of interlocking S's and C's that made her look like she would fit exactly against him if he were to embrace her. —Jeremy Dyson, *Never Trust a Rabbit*

I bent and slipped off my aunt's shoes, then stood back as she settled herself onto her side, her knees drawn up as much as age and arthritis would allow. Her thin body formed a wizened letter C in the center of the soft yellow sheet. —Kathryn R. Wall, *Perdition House: A Bay Tanner Mystery*

Houdini's tomb was the largest and most splendid in the cemetery, completely out of keeping with the general modesty, even austerity, of the other headstones and slabs. It was a curious structure, like a spacious balcony detached from the side of a palace, a letter C of marble balustrade with pillars like serifs at either end, enclosing a long low bench. —Michael Chabon, *The Amazing Adventures of Kavalier & Clay*

You know, we look like the letter C. We are very susceptible to a person of the opposite sex, some other circle half complete, coming up and joining with us—completing the circle that way—and giving us a burst of euphoria and energy that feels like the wholeness that a full connection with the universe produces. —James Redfield, *The Celestine Prophecy*

27. *n.* C post: "a C-shaped pillar on the side of a car, which connects the floor and roof." —Dr. John Burkardt

28. *n.* C clamp: a clamp in the shape of the letter C.

29. *n.* C-scroll: an ornamental design, as on furniture. *[T]he lower corners of the frame above the arch turn into C-scrolls with characteristic hawks' bills and acanthus swirls.* —Robert W. Berger, *A Royal Passion: Louis XIV as Patron of Architecture*

30. *n.* C-fold towels: "paper towels made by folding two opposite sides to meet in the middle, forming a sort of flat C." —Dr. John Burkardt

31. *n.* C spring: a coil of wire in the shape of the letter C.

32. *n.* C wrench: a wrench used to control the focus of a microscope.

SCIENTIFIC MATTERS

33. *n.* A vitamin (ascorbic acid).
    Vitamin C is widely reputed to prevent and/or cure the common cold. Although this has not been proved scientifically, it does help the body fight and resist infection. Like beta carotene and vitamin E, vitamin C is an antioxidant. It helps wounds heal, improves the body's absorption of iron, and is involved in the growth and maintenance of bones, teeth, gums, ligaments, and blood vessels. ... Vitamin C is found almost exclusively in fruits and vegetables, although breast milk and organ meats contain small amounts. Citrus fruits, tomatoes, peppers, strawberries, and cantaloupe are all excellent sources. —American Medical Association

34. *n.* (chemistry) The symbol for the element carbon in the periodic table.

35. *n.* (biology) Cytosine, one of the four nitrogenous bases found in DNA nucleotides.

36. *n.* (physics) The velocity of light *c* in vacuum as in Albert Einstein's relativity equation $E = mc^2$.

37. *n.* (electronics) A battery, as in "C supply."

38. *n.* A high-level programming language.
    Programmers based the C programming language on an early programming language by the name of B (although no programming language known as A

*ever existed). Programmers wanted to make pro-
gramming as easy as possible for themselves, so they
made the C programming language look more like
actual words that people can understand.* —Wallace
Wang, *Beginning Programming for Dummies*

39. *n.* A future event caused by something in the present.
    *[A] feeling of timelessness, the feeling that what we
    know as time is only the result of a naïve faith in
    causality—the notion that A in the past* caused *B in
    the present, which will* cause *C in the future.* —Tom
    Wolfe, *The Electric Kool-Aid Acid Test*

40. *n.* a high-level perception of cosmic unity, beyond
    causality.
    *[A]ctually A, B, and C are all part of a pattern
    that can be truly understood only by opening the
    doors of perception and experiencing it . . . in this
    moment . . . this supreme moment . . . this* kairos.
    —Tom Wolfe, *The Electric Kool-Aid Acid Test*

41. *n.* The active force in the cosmic property of a sub-
    stance.
    *When a substance is the conductor of the first or
    the active force, it is called "carbon," and, like the
    carbon of chemistry, it is designated by the letter C.*
    —P. D. Uspenskii, *In Search of the Miraculous: Frag-
    ments of an Unknown Teaching*

42. *n.* C horizon: the regolith layer of soil (beneath the
    subsoil) consisting of broken-up bedrock and very
    little organic matter.

C

D IN PRINT AND PROVERB

1. **(in literature)** *"He flung out in his violent way, and said with a D, 'Then do as you like.' "* —Charles Dickens, *Great Expectations.* The *D* here is a euphemism for *damn.*

2. **(in literature)** *"Boxer [the horse] could not get beyond the letter D."* —George Orwell, *Animal Farm*

3. **(in literature)** As a monogram: *" 'I can't help but notice the interesting design on your ring,' I told him. 'What do you call that?' 'I call it,' he said, 'the letter D.' "* —Vivian Vande Velde, *Heir Apparent*

4. **(in literature)** *"D is for lots of things."* —Neil Gaiman, *The Sandman: Preludes and Nocturnes*

5. **(in literature)** *"D is the human back."* —Victor Hugo, quoted in *ABZ* by Mel Gooding

6. *n.* A written representation of the letter.
   He would commence a letter with the words "Dear Sir," forming the letter "D" with painful, accurate slowness, elaborating and thickening the up and down strokes, and being troubled when he had to leave that letter for the next one; he built the next letter by hair strokes and would start on the third with hatred. —James Stephens, *The Crock of Gold*

7. *n.* A device, such as a printer's type, for reproducing the letter.

IN SHAPE

8. *n.* A semicircle on a pool table that is about twenty-two inches in diameter and is used in snooker games.

[T]he balls are arranged to begin, with the cueball in the D. —Robert Byrne, *Byrne's Wonderful World of Pool and Billiards: A Cornucopia of Instruction, Strategy, Anecdote, and Colorful Characters*

9. *n.* Something having the shape of a D.

10. *n.* A shoe width size (narrower than E, wider than C). *Most men's shoes are in a D width and women's in a B width.* —Joe Ellis, *Running Injury-Free: How to Prevent, Treat, and Recover from Dozens of Painful Problems*

11. *n.* A trotting pattern for horse training. *When the horse can trot the D, we are ready to pick up our lead.* —John Lyons, *Lyons on Horses: John Lyons' Proven Conditioned-Response Training Program*

12. *n.* D duct: a hot air duct whose cross-section is shaped like the letter D.

13. *n.* D net: a net "with an orifice shaped like a D, used for collecting plankton from the bottom of the ocean bed." —Dr. John Burkardt

14. *n.* D ring: "a metal ring in the shape of the letter D; the flat side commonly allows a strap to pass through." —Dr. John Burkardt

15. *n.* D valve: a metal D-shaped valve used in steam engines.

PLACEMENT

16. *n.* The fourth in a series.

17. *n.* A grade in school indicating "unsatisfactory."

Last year he got all A's on his report card and this year he's getting mostly D's and F's. We're so proud.
—Luke Rhinehart, *The Dice Man*

18. *n.* One graded with a D.
Many parents will resist abolishing letter grades because we grew up with them and apparently have an obsession with labeling each child an "A student" or a "D student." —Jeffrey Freed, *Right-Brained Children in a Left-Brained World: Unlocking the Potential of Your ADD Child*

19. *n.* A Roman numeral for 500.

20. *n.* Something arbitrarily designated D (e.g., a person, place, or other thing).

21. *n.* The saloon deck of the *Titanic.*
On most Titanic *floorplans, D is Saloon Deck.* —Chris Mcqueeny, "Encyclopedia Titanica" Message Board

MISCELLANEOUS

22. *n.* Any spoken sound represented by the letter.
The sound vibration of the consonant D means "doing, creating, creation, throwing light." —Joseph E. Rael, *Tracks of Dancing Light: A Native American Approach to Understanding Your Name*

23. *n.* The fourth letter of the alphabet.
In the days that followed, Lemprière wrestled with the letter "D." —Lawrence Norfolk, *Lemprière's Dictionary*
You might see yourself selling your gun to a gigantic letter D. —Harry Lorayne, *The Memory Book*

24. *n.* A group of artworks.

Representational and abstract elements were combined by Sam Gilliam in the D Series, in which the canvas is a three dimensional conversation with paint and the enigmatic hint of subject with the inclusion of a single letter. —Carolina Arts

MARKS AND BRANDS

25. *n.* A mark of shame for drunkards in Colonial America.
    Drunkards were forced to wear a great shame-letter D, "made of red cloth and set upon white, and to continue for a year." —David Hackett Fischer, Albion's Seed: Four British Folkways in America

26. *n.* The brand of a Civil War deserter.
    The letter D would be seared onto his buttock, his hip, or his cheek. It would be a letter one and a half inches high—the regulations became quite specific on this point—and it would either be burned on with a hot iron or cut with a razor and the wound filled with black powder, both to cause irritation and indelibility. —Simon Winchester, The Professor and the Madman: A Tale of Murder, Insanity, and the Making of "The Oxford English Dictionary"

27. *n.* A mark indicating "killed in combat."
    With a ballpoint pen, my best friend in Vietnam had written the letter D on the figure of every man that had been photographed for his album. D stood for dead and that singular tattoo was marked on all poses—sitting, standing, eating, or laughing. —D. S. Lliteras, Into the Ashes: A Novel

SCIENTIFIC MATTERS

28. *n.* A vitamin (cholecalciferol).

Vitamin D works with calcium to build strong bones
and teeth and maintain the nervous system.... For most
people, sun exposure is the primary source of vitamin D.
Food sources include vitamin D–fortified milk, eggs, fish
liver oils, and fatty fish such as herring, mackerel, and
salmon. —American Medical Association

29. *n.* (biology) Aspartate, an amino acid.

30. *n.* A layer of the ionosphere, as in the "D layer."
[The D layer is the] lowest part of the ionosphere,
which appears at an altitude of 50–80km. This layer
has a negative effect on radio waves, because it only
absorbs radio-energy. It develops shortly after sun-
rise and disappears shortly after sunrise. This layer
reaches maximum ionization when the sun is at its
highest point in the sky. —WWDX Propagation College

EXERTIONS OF POWER

31. *n.* A planned attack, as in "D-Day."
"D-Day" is a military term designating the start
date for launching an operation, but in modern
history it generally refers to the events of June 6th
1944. —D-Day Museum

32. *n.* (physics) A state of atomic energy.

SYMPHONY IN D

33. *n.* The second note in a C-major musical scale.

34. *n.* A written or printed representation of a
musical note D.

D

35. *n.* A string, key, or pipe tuned to the note D.

36. *n.* The fourth section in a piece of music.
   *We came to grief a few bars after letter D, where solo
   passages for woodwinds are mated to triadic figura-
   tions in the piano part, and Stokowski signaled a halt.*
   —Glenn Gould, *The Glenn Gould Reader*

37. *n.* D hole: a D-shaped sound hole in a guitar or viol.

CONTRACTION 'D

38. *v.* Had. *He'd better do it.*

39. *v.* Did. *How'd she do that?*

40. *v.* Would. *I'd like to go.*

41. *v.* (informal) Do or did. *How d'you take your coffee?*

FOREIGN MEANINGS

42. *adj.* (German) Through, as in *D-Zug,* a through or
   express train.

43. *v.* (French) (slang) To wangle, as in *Employer
   le système D.*

44. *n.* (Hebrew) The letter *D* is called *daleth,* which
   means "a door."

E IN PRINT AND PROVERB

1. (phrase) This may be inscribed in a church under the two tablets of the Ten Commandments: "PRSVR PRFCT MN VR KP THS PRCPTS TN. The Vowel E Supplies the Key."

2. (phrase) *To give the big E* means to brush off or ignore. The *E* originally stood for *elbow.*

3. (in literature) *"E, candor of steam and of tents, /Lances of proud glaciers, white kings, Queen-Anne's-lace shivers."* —Arthur Rimbaud, "Vowels"

4. (in literature) French author Georges Perec wrote an entire book, *La Disparition,* without using the letter *E.* This book was translated into English, also without the *E,* under the title *A Void.*

5. (in literature) *"The peninsular landscape is full of contrasts, paradoxes, and transformations. The most prominent elements on the horizon are forever silent, while smaller outgrowths have a profound resonance. More amazing, though, is how proximity to an E can actually transform an object into something entirely different. (Luckily, as my name is Sam, I remained the same.) I have sketched a rough map of the terrain, but have yet to fill in the details. I'm in no hurry, as the landscape of E will remain forever etched in my memory."* —Craig Conley, *The Workbook of One-Letter Words*

6. (in literature) The title of a seven-minute Canadian animated film directed by Bretislav Pojar. *A giant statue of the letter "E" arrives in the park. One man sees it as "B"; they are preparing to cart him off to the loony bin when a doctor arrives and determines the man needs glasses. Then the king*

arrives; he also sees "B." He tries on the glasses, sees "E," and pins a medal on the doctor then has his goon squad come and bash on everyone's head until they too see "B." —Anonymous

7. (in literature) " 'That's half of the Electric Palace symbol,' Cal said. The Electric Palace was an electronic store in Odyssey. 'The E is missing, but that's it.' " —Marshall Younger, *Mysteries in Odyssey #1: Case of the Mysterious Message*

8. (in literature) *"E is the foundations, the pillar, the console, and the architrave, all architecture in a single letter."* —Victor Hugo, quoted in *ABZ* by Mel Gooding.

9. (in popular usage) *"E-nough already! The 'E' has come to be the favored letter in the e-world of Silicon Valley. Have they forgotten about the other 25 perfectly good characters of the alphabet? Let us start with the vowels that have been left to collect dust as their compatriot has made its meteoric rise to fame. What of 'A'—was this not your first vowel, bringing to mind fond childhood memories of ABCs and 123s? What of 'I'—that character that embodies the self and so much more? What of 'O'—which is in itself a perfect exclamation of any and all emotions? What of 'U'—counterpart to 'I' that gives it balance and brings community? And sometimes 'Y'—ever questioning and pushing the boundaries? Does not the power of the 'E' pale when placed next to the stunning expansiveness of the other vowels? We do not seek the demise of our friend 'E,' but merely want to put it in its place, and provide an environment in which all the other letters have room to grow and flourish.* —Anton Vowl, The Society for the Preservation of the Other 25 Letters of the Alphabet

10. *n.* A written representation of the letter.
"Make lots of Es," she urged them. "E is one of the most important letters there is." Mrs. Michaels wrote the letter E on five different little pieces of paper. —Johanna Hurwitz, *E Is for Elisa*

11. *n.* A device, such as a printer's type, for reproducing the letter.

FROM ONE TO FIVE

12. *n.* One piece of Styrofoam packing material (in the shape of an E).

13. *n.* In England, the second-class Lloyd's rating for the quality of a merchant ship.

14. *n.* One of four cardinal points on a compass (**abbreviation for East**).

15. *n.* The fifth in a series.

LEVELS OF ACHIEVEMENT

16. *n.* A U.S. government award (usually a pennant bearing an E, symbolizing excellence) given to an industrial organization.

17. *n.* A grade in school indicating "excellent."
The grading system used during most of the period before 1928 would appear confusing when compared to what is used today. For many years, students were given four possible grades: E for excellent, G for good, F for fair, and P for poor. —Gerald F. De Jong, *From Strength to Strength: A History of Northwestern, 1882–1982*

18. *n.* One graded with an E.

MUSIC

19. *n.* A written or printed representation of a musical note E.

    He stayed for the second encore—an otherwise inspiring version of Finlandia, *sunk by the incapacity of the aforementioned hornist, Mr. Kelleher, to hit a good E-flat.* —Brooks Hansen, *Perlman's Ordeal*

20. *n.* A string, key, or pipe tuned to the note E.

21. *n.* The fifth section in a piece of music.

    Beginning with the letter E, that is, the main section of the first movement [of Nikolai Sidelnikov's symphony The Duels*], the series is a kind of sound "matrix" consisting of thirteen sounds, where twelve are changed and the thirteenth is a "random one" which introduces an element of free development.* —M. Lobanova, *Musical Style and Genre: History and Modernity*

22. *n.* The third note in a C-major musical scale.

MISCELLANEOUS

23. *n.* The fifth letter of the alphabet.

    It was a promiscuous, fawning surd, continually merging with its neighboring consonants ("R" in particular), confirming Lemprière's view of [E] as a perdifious little hieroglyph. —Lawrence Norfolk, *Lemprière's Dictionary*

    What is the beginning of the end, the end of the infinite, and the beginning of eternity? Answer: the letter e. —Mark Barrenechea, *Software Rules: How the Next Generation of Enterprise Applications Will Increase Strategic Effectiveness*

24. *n.* Any spoken sound represented by the letter.
   The sound vibration of the vowel E means "reflec-
   tion, reflectivity, relationship, placing, placement,
   grid, mirror, echo." —Joseph E. Rael, *Tracks of*
   Dancing Light: A Native American Approach to
   Understanding Your Name

25. *n.* Something having the shape of an E.
   He had decided on the "E" shape for the building to
   keep it narrow enough to maximize the efficient use
   of natural light and because, had it run end to end
   in a line, the amount of floor space required would
   have made the building too long. —Vicki Boatright,
   The Panama Canal Review

26. *n.* A Roman numeral for 250.

27. *n.* Something arbitrarily designated E (e.g., a person, place, or other thing).

28. *n.* A shoe width size (narrower than EE, wider
   than D).

29. *n.* (logic) The notation of a universal negative
   statement, such as "no plants are mammals."
   In categorical logic, the square of opposition
   describes the relationship between the universal
   affirmative *A*, the universal negative *E*, the particular affirmative *I*, and the particular negative *O*.

30. *n.* (mathematics) The natural number *e*, used as
   the base for natural logarithms and with applica-
   tions in problems of population growth and radioactive decay.

31. *n.* The heaviest weight of sandpaper available.
   [T]he letter E denotes the heaviest [weight of paper
   used]. —Bruce E. Johnson, *The Wood Finisher*

SCIENTIFIC MATTERS

32. *n.* A vitamin (tocepherol).
    Vitamin E is a key player in the body's defense system. An antioxidant, it protects the lungs, nervous system, skeletal muscle, and the eye's retina from damage by free radicals (cell-damaging chemicals). It also protects cell membranes and is believed to slow aging of cells. It helps form red blood cells and protects them from being destroyed. It may also reduce the risk of heart disease by protecting against atherosclerosis (the buildup of fat in the arteries), but this has not yet been proved conclusively.... Vitamin E is found in vegetable oils, nuts, wheat germ and whole-wheat products, egg yolks, and green leafy vegetables. —American Medical Association

33. *n.* (chemistry) The symbol for the element einsteinium in the periodic table.

34. *n.* (physics) The fundamental unit of charge e, originally measured by Robert Millikan in 1917, was later refined through the discovery of the relationship between the Avogadro's constant N and the Faraday constant F.

35. *n.* (biology) Glutamate, an amino acid.

36. *n.* A layer of the ionosphere, as in the "E layer."
    This part of the ionosphere is located just above the D-layer at an altitude of 90–130km. This layer can only reflect radio waves up to about 5MHz. It has a negative effect on 27MHz, due to absorption of radio waves above 5MHz. It develops shortly after sunset, and disappears a few hours after sunset. Maximum ionization is reached around midday. —WWDX Propagation College

37. *n.* The numerical value of pi.
    Cajori writes that "perhaps the earliest use of a single letter to represent the ratio of the length of a circle to its diameter" occurs in 1689 in Mathesis enucleata by J. Christoph Sturm, who used e for 3.14159. —Jeff Miller, "Earliest Uses of Various Mathematical Symbols"

38. *n.* A number whose hyperbolic logarithm is equal to 1, adopted by Leonhard Euler in 1736.
    Why did he choose the letter e? There is no general consensus. According to one view, Euler chose it because it is the first letter of the word exponential. More likely, the choice came to him naturally as the first "unused" letter of the alphabet, since the letters a, b, c, and d frequently appear elsewhere in mathematics. It seems unlikely that Euler chose the letter because it is the initial of his own name, as occasionally been suggested: he was an extremely modest man and often delayed publication of his own work so that a colleague or student of his would get due credit. In any event, his choice of the symbol e, like so many other symbols of his, became universally accepted. —Eli Maor, quoted in Jeff Miller, "Earliest Uses of Various Mathematical Symbols"

39. *n.* E horizon: the eluviation layer of the soil (beneath the topsoil) consisting of silt and sand but few minerals.

FOREIGN MEANINGS

40. *prep.* (Latin) Out of; as in *E pluribus unum,* "one out of many."

FACTS AND FIGURES

41. *E* is the most commonly occurring of all letters. *A* is third, *O* fourth, *I* fifth, and *U* comes in a distant twelfth.

F IN PRINT AND PROVERB

1. **(in film)** The title of a film from the Czech Republic, written and directed by Janja Glogovac.

2. **(in literature)** *"F is the gibbet."* —Victor Hugo, quoted in *ABZ* by Mel Gooding

3. The letter *F* is so associated with the vulgar "f-word" that the very sight of it, even out of any context, can suggest the vulgarity.
The [Ouija] board quivered again and the girls hushed. It moved, stopped, moved again. It made the letter F. "Fuh..." the girl named Sandy said. "Fuck you, too," someone else said, and they were off and giggling again. —Stephen King, *The Stand*

4. *n.* A written representation of the letter.
The white corner painted on the floor was being revealed as part of a word. It was the top of the capital letter F. —Barbara D'Amato, *Help Me Please*

5. *n.* A device, such as a printer's type, for reproducing the letter.

LAYERS AND LEVELS

6. *n.* A layer of the ionosphere, as in the "F layer."
The F-layer appears a few hours after sunset, when the F1- and F2-layers merge. The F-layer is located between 250–500km altitude. Even well into the night, this layer may reflect radio waves up to 20 MHz, and occasionally even up to 25 MHz. —WWDX Propagation College

7. *n.* The sixth in a series.

8. *n.* A nonpassing grade in school indicating "failing." *Not enough comments on it, insufficient explanation of her F.* —William H. Gass, *The Tunnel*

9. *n.* One graded with an F. *an F student*

KEYS AND SCALES

10. *n.* The fourth note in a C-major musical scale.

11. *n.* A written or printed representation of a musical note F.

12. *n.* A string, key, or pipe tuned to the note F.

13. *n.* The sixth section in a piece of music.

14. *n.* F hole: "the long graceful curly openings on the faces of violins and certain other stringed instruments, shaped like a baroque *f*." —Dr. John Burkardt

15. *n.* A notation meaning "clef" in the earliest surviving written music of medieval European chants (about the year 1000). *The letter F at the beginning of the line was called a Clef, because it was a key, or clue, to the knowledge of the level of sound.* —Imogen Holst, *ABC of Music: A Short Practical Guide to the Basics*

MISCELLANEOUS

16. *n.* The sixth letter of the alphabet. *Take the F from life and you have lie.* —James Thurber, "The Wonderful O" *[A]s I was looking through a microscope at a tropical moth, to my surprise I noticed a tiny, perfect*

letter F hidden on the wing. I was astounded and wondered if I could find other letters. . . . Little did I imagine that it would take more than twenty-five years and visits to more than thirty countries to discover all the letters of the alphabet. —Kjell B. Sandved, *The Butterfly Alphabet*

*He flipped to the back of the book, intending to look under the letter F for titles containing the word fuòco—*fire—*but the F's were not together. Langdon swore under his breath.* What the hell do these people have against alphabetizing? —Dan Brown, *Angels and Demons*

17. *n.* Any spoken sound represented by the letter.
The sound vibration of the consonant F means "faith." —Joseph E. Rael, *Tracks of Dancing Light: A Native American Approach to Understanding Your Name*
The letter f is more like a breath blown out between the lips. —Jarrell D. Sieff, *A Practical Guide to Living in Japan: Everything You Need to Know to Successfully Settle In*

18. *n.* Feather.
You could have knocked me down with a f. —P. G. Wodehouse, *Right Ho, Jeeves*

19. *n.* Something having the shape of an F.
The Okinawans used a type of halter on those horses that I had never seen before. It consisted of two pieces of wood held in place by ropes. The wooded pieces on either side of the horse's head were shaped like the letter F. —Eugene B. Sledge, *With the Old Breed: At Peleliu and Okinawa*

20. *n.* Something designated F.
Books you were going to write with letters for titles. Have you read his F? O yes, but I prefer Q. Yes, but W is wonderful. O yes, W. —James Joyce, *Ulysses*

21. *n.* Someone called F.
Uncle F left me a small landscape painting I'd once admired. —Iain Banks, *The Business*

22. *n.* A medieval Roman numeral for 40.

23. *n.* Something arbitrarily designated F (e.g., a person, place, or other thing).

24. *n.* Something arbitrarily called F that takes on significance depending upon context.
We have arbitrarily chosen the letter "F" for a certain purpose, so that "Fx" shall have a certain meaning (depending on x). As a result of this choice "F," previously non-significant, becomes significant; it has meaning. But it is clearly an impossible simplification to suppose that there is a single object F, which it means. —F. P. Ramsey, "The Foundations of Mathematics," *F. P. Ramsey: Philosophical Papers*

SCIENTIFIC MATTERS

25. *n.* (chemistry) The symbol for the element fluorine in the periodic table.

26. *n.* (physics) The Faraday constant *F* equals the amount of charge that must pass through a solution to electrolytically deposit a mole of a singly charged, or monovalent, element contained in the solution.

27. *n.* (physics) A state of atomic energy.

28. *n.* (biology) Phenylalanine, an amino acid.

29. *n.* (astronomy) A class of stars in between white and yellow.

30. *n.* (mechanics) F head: "Having one valve in the head, and another on the side of the engine cylinder."
—Dr. John Burkardt

FACTS AND FIGURES

31. Until 1822, the letter F (for "fray-maker") was branded on the cheeks of people who fought in church.

G IN PRINT AND PROVERB

1. **(in literature)** *"He harkens after prophecies and dreams, and from the cross-row plucks the letter G. And says a wizard told him, that by G his issue disinherited should be."* —**William Shakespeare,** *Richard III,* I.i.54–56

2. **(in literature)** *G* is a 1980 novel by John Berger.

3. **(in literature)** *"[N]ow the bloody old lunatic is gone round to Green street to look for a G man."* —**James Joyce,** *Ulysses.* Here, *G* stands for *government.*

4. **(in literature)** As a marker of sobriety: *"Even before she was out of the car, the trooper asked Linda to recite the alphabet, starting with the letter G. It occurred to her that starting with G instead of A was supposed to rattle someone who was already disoriented from having too much to drink."* —**Marlene Steinberg,** *The Stranger in the Mirror*

5. **(in literature)** *"G is the French horn."* —**Victor Hugo,** quoted in *ABZ* by Mel Gooding

6. ***n.* (slang)** One thousand dollars.
   [Walt] still owes me two G's and he's out at the Doll House the other night, stuffing twenties into the girls' G-strings. —Peter Blauner, *The Intruder*

7. ***n.* (slang)** A word used to address a friend.
   Yah, what g? —*The Rap Dictionary*

8. **(contraction)** Good, as in "g'day."

9. ***n.*** A written representation of the letter.
   If I were to plead trouble with any letter it would probably be the g, a mere "twiddle" of the pen at

best, but a delightful twiddle nevertheless.
—Frederic Goudy, type designer
He died on the ninth of October, the day that the
single letter G appeared on the wall of his room
facing his bed, and on the twenty-fifth day of his
illness. —Robert Graves, *I, Claudius*

10. *n.* A device, such as a printer's type, for reproducing the letter.

MUSIC

11. *n.* The fifth note in a C-major musical scale.
    The middle G was sticking, but still he recognized
    the theme. —Brooks Hansen, *Perlman's Ordeal*
    It was a piano note, G, perfectly formed in perfect
    pitch, a universe created by the oscillation of a
    string in the air. —Pat Cadigan, *Mindplayers*

12. *n.* A written or printed representation of a
    musical note G.

13. *n.* A string, key, or pipe tuned to the note G.

14. *n.* The seventh section in a piece of music.

G-RATED G-STRINGS

15. *n.* A loincloth, as in a G-string.
    The earliest known reference to G-string is in
    J. H. Beadles' Western Wilds, written circa 1878:
    "Around each boy's waist is the tight 'geestring,'
    from which a single strip of cloth runs between the
    limbs from front to back." From this we see that
    G-string originally referred only to the thong
    around the waist, which is precisely what a "girdle"

G

was in its earliest form. Thus G-string may be an abbreviation of "girdlestring," the only difficulty being that no such word has ever come to light, that I am aware of, anyway. Alternatively, we may note that "string" was a common 19th-century synonym for "whip," which was of the same rawhide construction as the aforementioned prairie G-string, and that "gee" is an expletive frequently employed to accelerate one's horse. A "geestring" may thus have been a pioneer horsewhip later discovered to be useful in holding up one's pants, or the equivalent thereof. Finally, and rather unimaginatively, we may observe that a G-string (the string part, that is) bears a superficial likeness to the fiddle string of similar designation. —Cecil Adams, *The Straight Dope*

16. *adj.* A rating for motion pictures acceptable for all age groups. (See *R, X.*)

MISCELLANEOUS

17. *n.* The seventh letter of the alphabet.
Governali . . . believes in History with the great H (indeed, in greatness itself with a great G).
—William H. Gass, *The Tunnel*
If you can't get the letter G out of your head because it keeps intruding itself forcefully while you're awaiting "genuine" impressions, say so.
—Laura Day, *Practical Intuition: How to Harness the Power of Your Instinct and Make It Work for You*

18. *n.* Any spoken sound represented by the letter.
The sound vibration of the consonant G means "goodness, God." —Joseph E. Rael, *Tracks of Dancing Light: A Native American Approach to Understanding Your Name*

*[Instead of calling my mother "Ma,"] I called her
Mag because for me, without my knowing why, the
letter g abolished the syllable Ma, and as it were
spat on it, better than any other letter would have
done.* —Samuel Beckett, *Molloy*

19. *n.* (slang) Glance.
    *I could see at a g. that the unfortunate affair
    had got in amongst her in no uncertain manner.*
    —P. G. Wodehouse, *Right Ho, Jeeves*

20. *n.* A Roman numeral for 400.

21. *n.* The seventh in a series.

22. *n.* A general factor in intelligence.
    [The authors of The Bell Curve *failed to justify their
    claim] that the number known as g, the celebrated
    "general factor" of intelligence, first identified by
    the British psychologist Charles Spearman, in 1904,
    captures a real property in the head.* —Steven Fra-
    ser, *The Bell Curve Wars: Race, Intelligence, and the
    Future of America*

23. *n.* Something arbitrarily designated G (e.g., a person,
    place, or other thing).

24. *n.* A designated location.
    *The two men filed to their seats, Perlman's—row
    G, a step up from last year's and slightly farther to
    the left, the better to see the hands of the pianist.*
    —Brooks Hansen, *Perlman's Ordeal*

25. *n.* The sign of a gossiper.
    *Isn't it against the law to gossip, even about
    witches? Don't you have to wear the letter G around
    your neck? I see two such letters in the courtroom.*
    —Sid Fleischman, *The 13th Floor*

26. *n.* Something having the shape of a G.
Staring at the worms, they tried to classify the
shapes. They saw snakes, pigtails, branchy, forked
things that looked like the letter Y, and they noticed
squiggles like a small g, and bends like the letter U.
—Richard Preston, *The Hot Zone*

SCIENTIFIC MATTERS

27. *n.* A vitamin (riboflavin). Also known as vitamin B2.

28. *n.* (electronics) Conductance, or the ability of a
material to pass electrons.
Conductance is symbolized by the capital letter G.
—Stan Gibilisco, *Teach Yourself Electricity and*
Electronics

29. *n.* (physics) The Newtonian gravitational constant
G was first measured in the eighteenth century by
Henry Cavendish and is a critical component of
the law of gravitation. G should be contrasted with
the gravitational acceleration constant *g*, which
Galileo demonstrated to be the acceleration rate of
any object (regardless of mass) due to gravity near
the Earth's surface.

30. *n.* (biology) Guanine, one of the four nitrogenous
bases found in DNA nucleotides.

31. *n.* (physics) A unit of force applied to a body when
accelerated, equal to the force exerted on the body
by gravity near the Earth's surface.
Nine Gs is about the maximum [amount of accelera-
tion that can be withstood by] human beings. At 9
Gs, most will black out after a few tenths of seconds.
Since most modern jet fighters can pull at least 9 Gs
in a tight turn, this is a serious problem for the Air

Force. The early manned-space flight program used to launch astronauts at 9 Gs, the Mercury, Gemini, and Apollo programs. The space shuttle is launched at a "comfortable" 3 Gs. —U.S. Department of Energy

32. *n.* A moment's will; an act of will.
We get the value of G by multiplying the will data rate by the consciousness time tick. —Evan Harris, *The Physics of Consciousness: The Quantum Mind and the Meaning of Life*

33. *n.* (astronomy) A class of yellow stars.
The letter G is used for our own sun and other yellow stars. —Dennis Richard Danielson, *The Book of the Cosmos*

34. *n.* (mechanics) G crimp: the British analog to a C clamp.

G

H IN PRINT AND PROVERB

1. **(in literature)** *"Beatrice: Heigh-ho! Margaret: For a hawk, a horse, or a husband? Beatrice: For the letter that begins them all, H."* —**William Shakespeare,** *Much Ado About Nothing,* III.iv.54–56. There is a pun here on *ache,* which in Shakespeare's day was pronounced *aitch.*

2. **(in literature)** *"I had a wound here that was like a T, but now 'tis made an H."* —**William Shakespeare,** *Antony and Cleopatra,* IV.vii.8. There is a pun here on *ache,* which in Shakespeare's day was pronounced *aitch.*

3. **(in literature)** *"H is a facade with two towers."* —Victor Hugo, quoted in *ABZ* by Mel Gooding

4. *n.* A written representation of the letter.
   With relief he fixed his eyes on some symbols pencilled on the wall inside: the letter H, and under it a row of figures. —Graham Greene, *The Heart of the Matter*
   The pencil moved beneath the painstaking coaxing of her fingers. She drew the letter h. Her hand was shaking so badly, she dropped the pencil. . . . Tate went after it. . . . He replaced the pencil in her hand and guided it back onto the tablet. "H what?" —Sandra Brown, *Mirror Image*

5. *n.* A device, such as a printer's type, for reproducing the letter.

MUSIC

6. *n.* In music, the German name for the note B-natural.

7. *n.* The eighth section in a piece of music.
   Only in the final section H [of Mozart's Le nozze
   di Figaro] *does the music build up to the torrent of
   noise described by Da Ponte.* —Andrew Steptoe,
   *The Mozart–Da Ponte Operas: The Cultural and
   Musical Background to "Le Nozze Di Figaro," "Don
   Giovanni," and "Cosi Fan Tutte"*

PEOPLE, PLACES, AND THINGS

8. *n.* Something arbitrarily designated H (e.g., a person, place, or other thing).

9. *n.* Someone called H.
   How bad is he, Miss H? —Iain Banks, *The Business*

10. *n.* The eighth in a series.
    *The defense of the city had been organized into
    eight sectors, designated by the letters A to H.*
    —Antony Beevor, *The Fall of Berlin 1945*

11. *n.* Something having the shape of an H, such as a grooved wooden plank.

12. *n.* A designated location.
    *He escorted her into room H, which was behind his
    office.* —Brooks Hansen, *Perlman's Ordeal*

MISCELLANEOUS

13. *n.* The eighth letter of the alphabet.
    *Governali . . . believes in History with the great
    H (indeed, in greatness itself with a great G).*
    —William H. Gass, *The Tunnel*
    *Think about it: one man's personal obsession with
    a more or less arbitrary letter of the alphabet has
    spread to the point where several generations of*

*Canadian poets have internalized it as their own. H
is the shiniest toy in the box, and everybody wants it.*
—Darren Wershler-Henry, *Nickolodeon*
*[N]o computer can handle the letter H by itself. It can
only handle numbers, so we have a convention that
the letter H will be represented by some number, such
as 72.* —Peter Gulutzan, *SQL-99 Complete, Really*

14. *n.* H beam: a metal beam whose cross-section is
H-shaped.
*The [Santa Barbara, California] pier was sup-
ported by 340 H-beam steel pilings.* —Nelson G.
Hairston, *Ecological Experiments: Purpose, Design,
and Execution*

15. *n.* H block: the H-shaped buildings in Maze Prison
(Ireland).
*You'll see lots of green Hs attached to lamp posts (in
memory of the H-blocks at the Maze prison where
the hunger strikers were incarcerated.* —Tom
Downs, *Lonely Planet: Ireland*

16. *n.* H budding: "plate budding in which cuts in the
bark of the stock are made in the form of an H."
—Dr. John Burkardt

17. *n.* A Roman numeral for 200.

18. *n.* H hinge: a hinge with H-shaped leaves.
*The earliest . . . [Shaker] interior doors featured
handwrought H-hinges screwed directly to the
face of the door and the face of the adjacent frame.*
—Christian Becksvoort, *The Shaker Legacy: Per-
spectives on an Enduring Furniture Style*

19. *n.* Any spoken sound represented by the letter.
*The sound vibration of the consonant H means
"stepladder to the heavenly planes, beyond the
beyond."* —Joseph E. Rael, *Tracks of Dancing Light:*

*A Native American Approach to Understanding
Your Name
That "orrible" omission of the letter h from places
where it ought to be, that aspiration of the h until
you exasperate it altogether—you cannot tell what
harm such mistakes may cause.* —C. H. Spurgeon,
*The Soulwinner
When the teacher called, "H-h-h-h," only the letter H
came back.* —Jean Feldman, *Teaching Tunes Audio-
tape and Mini-Books Set: Early Phonics*

20. *n.* H stretcher: "a bar supporting two other bars
and forming an H; often seen in chair legs."
—Dr. John Burkardt

SCIENTIFICALLY SPEAKING

21. *n.* A vitamin (biotin).
*Found in every cell in the body, biotin is an essen-
tial growth factor. It is involved in the enzyme
action that enables protein and carbohydrate
metabolism, the breakdown of fatty acids, and the
synthesis of DNA in cells. . . . Foods rich in biotin
include oats, organ meats, yeast, and eggs (cooked);
smaller amounts are found in whole-wheat products, dairy products, fish, and tomatoes.* —American Medical Association
*And it doesn't really matter, anyway, because we'll
soon fatten him up again. All we'll have to do is give
him a triple dosage of my wonderful Supervitamin
Chocolate. Supervitamin Chocolate contains huge
amounts of vitamin A and vitamin B. It also contains
vitamin C, vitamin D, vitamin E, vitamin F, vitamin
G, vitamin I, vitamin J, vitamin K, vitamin L, vitamin
M, vitamin N, vitamin O, vitamin P, vitamin Q, vitamin
R, vitamin T, vitamin U, vitamin V, vitamin W, vitamin
X, vitamin Y, and, believe it or not, vitamin Z! The*

only two vitamins it doesn't have in it are vitamin S, because it makes you sick, and vitamin H, because it makes you grow horns on the top of your head, like a bull. But it does have a very small amount of the rarest and most magical vitamin of them all—vitamin Wonka.
—Roald Dahl, *Charlie and the Chocolate Factory*

22. *n.* The horizontal component of the total intensity of a magnetic field, measured in units of nanoTesla. The Earth's magnetic field intensity is roughly between 25,000 and 65,000 nT.

23. *n.* The cosmic property of a substance without relation to the force manifesting itself through it. *When a substance is taken without relation to the force manifesting itself through it, it is called "hydrogen," and, like the hydrogen of chemistry, it is designated by the letter H.* —P. D. Uspenskii, *In Search of the Miraculous: Fragments of an Unknown Teaching*

24. *n.* (physics) The Planck constant h is the proportion between the total energy and frequency of a photon (a single quantum unit of electromagnetic energy such as light or heat radiation).

25. *n.* (thermodynamics) Enthalpy. The internal energy of a system can be divided into two parts: the capacity to do pressure-volume work and the capacity to transfer heat, known as enthalpy H.

26. *n.* (chemistry) The symbol for the element hydrogen in the periodic table.
"Think you could swim in heavy water?" "H two O two? Very buoyantly, I imagine." —Iain Banks, *The Business*

27. *n.* (anatomy) The gray matter in the center of the spinal cord.

The posterior (dorsal) horns are gray matter areas
at the rear of each side of the H.... The lateral horns
are small projections of gray matter at the sides of
H. —Phillip E. Pack, *Anatomy and Physiology*

FOREIGN MEANINGS

28. *n.* (French) Zero, as in *L'heure H,* "zero hour."

I IN PRINT AND PROVERB

1. (phrase) *I per se:* the letter I by itself makes a word.

2. (phrase) *"I came, I saw, I conquered."* —Julius Caesar

3. (chiefly obsolete) Aye.

4. (in literature) *"Hath Romeo slain himself? Say thou but ay, and that bare vowel I shall poison more than the death-darting eye of cockatrice. I am not I, if there be such an ay, or those eyes shut, that makes thee answer ay."* —William Shakespeare, *Romeo and Juliet,* III.ii.45–49. The wordplay here is on *I, ay,* and *eye.*

5. (in literature) *"I, deep reds, spit blood, laughter of beautiful lips/In anger or in drunkenness and penitence."* —Arthur Rimbaud, "Vowels"

6. (in literature) *"I is the first letter of the alphabet, the first word of the language, the first thought of the mind, the first object of affection."* —Ambrose Bierce, *Collected Writings*

7. (in literature) *"And now I see the face of god, and I raised this god over the earth, this god whom men have sought since men came into being, this god who will grant them joy and peace and pride. This god, this one word: 'I.' "* —Ayn Rand, *Anthem*

8. (in literature) *"I . . . how huge a word in that small English mark, the shape of a Grecian pillar."* —William H. Gass, *The Tunnel*

9. (in literature) *"I is the war machine launching a projectile."* —Victor Hugo, quoted in *ABZ* by Mel Gooding

10. *n.* A written representation of the letter.

If a one letter word is found for a ciphertext of a formal English message, it is obvious that the letter is either an I or an A. —Al Court, *An Introduction to Cryptography.* In fact, this claim is false, as this dictionary proves.

When a schoolteacher writes "I" on a blackboard and asks the students what they see, most of them will answer that they see the word "I." It's rare for someone to say "I see a blackboard with 'I' written on it." Just as the relatively huge blackboard is ignored in favor of a single letter, we ignore the Awareness that is the permanent background to all phenomena." —Leo Hartong, *Awakening to the Dream*

11. *n.* A device, such as a printer's type, for reproducing the letter.

LOOKING OUT FOR NUMBER ONE

12. *n.* The ego, self.

The ego, that whole construct we so easily name "I," also has its less than appealing needs. —Thomas Moore, *Care of the Soul*

The words that really matter in the English language are the little words, and the shorter the word the greater its significance, it seems. The most important word in our language is a one-letter word. I is the supreme example of the importance of short words. Not only is it a single letter, but it is always a capital letter. It stands symmetrical and alone, head and shoulders above almost all other words in a written sentence. I is the most commonly used word in everyday speech. I is the point from which we see and experience the world. It is the subject of the sentence, and me, the objective case of I, is a two-letter word that is not far behind in significance. —Dr. Michael Houseley, *Medical Post*

13. *n.* An especially egotistic person who uses the first person pronoun excessively. *He's just a big* I.

14. *n.* A dichotomous part of one's self. *the other* I
What a lot of phenomenological ambitions would be necessary to uncover the "I" of different states corresponding to different narcotics! At the very least, it would be necessary to classify these "I's" in three species: the "I" of sleep—if it exists; the "I" of the narcosis—if it retains any value as individuality; the "I" of reverie, maintained in such vigilance that it can permit itself the happiness of writing.... Is there an "I" which assumes these multiple "I's"? An "I" of all these "I's" which has the mastery of our whole being, of all our intimate beings? Novalis writes: ["The supreme task of culture is to take possession of its transcendental self, to be at once the I of its I."] If the "I's" vary in tonality of being, where is the dominant "I"? In looking for the "I" of the "I's" won't we find, by dreaming like Novalis, the "I" of the "I," the transcendental "I"? —Gaston Bachelard, *The Poetics of Reverie: Childhood, Language, and the Cosmos*

15. *n.* A Roman numeral for one. (See *J*.)

16. *n.* something arbitrarily designated I (e.g., a person, place, or other thing).

17. *pronoun.* Nominative singular pronoun.
Our practice of capitalizing the first person singular pronoun—I—is also bizarrely tied in with the badly understood conventions of when to write Roman I with a tail and when to leave well enough alone. —Alexander Humez, *A B C Et Cetera*

18. *pronoun.* Narrator of a literary work written in the first person singular.

I started performing on the world stage with a borrowed silver spoon in my mouth. —Michael York, *Accidentally on Purpose*

MISCELLANEOUS

19. *n.* The ninth letter of the alphabet.
Colossal edifice denoted by one-letter word: /Remove "I" from pain and become Pan. —K.P. Kaligari, "Moina, My Reflection"

20. *n.* Something having the shape of an I.

21. *n.* I beam: a steel joist or girder whose cross-section is I-shaped.
Imagine that you and I are standing in a room at opposite ends of a 120-foot steel I-beam, the type that's used in construction. I pull a hundred-dollar bill from my wallet and shout—120 feet is a long way—"Hey, you down at the end! If you'll walk the length of this I-beam in two minutes without stepping off the other side, I'll give you a hundred dollars!" Would you come? It's your own choice, of course, but I'll bet you're already on that beam. —Hyrum W. Smith, *Priorities Magazine*

22. *n.* Any spoken sound represented by the letter.
The sound vibration of the vowel I means "awareness." —Joseph E. Rael, *Tracks of Dancing Light: A Native American Approach to Understanding Your Name*

23. *n.* A grade in school indicating a student's work is incomplete.
Although we tried a variety of strategies to promote greater success . . . many students still had grades of D or F or took an incomplete (I) in at least one of their classes —Ruth Schoenbach, *Reading for Understanding*

24. *n.* The ninth in a series.

25. *n.* The ninth section in a piece of music.

26. *n.* I bar: a steel beam whose cross-section is I-shaped.

27. *n.* I girder: a steel beam whose cross-section is I-shaped, used as a structural support in buildings or bridges.
An investigation uncovered improper reinforcement in the flanges of precast concrete I-girders that supported the double-tee roof deck. —Jacob Feld, *Construction Failure*

28. *n.* I hat: a cap with a floppy brim.

29. *n.* I iron: a steel beam whose cross-section is I-shaped.

30. *n.* I ring: a metal band encircling a metal drum.

31. *n.* I formation: "an offensive football play in which the quarterback, a half back, the full back, and the tail back line up behind the center." —Dr. John Burkardt

SCIENTIFIC MATTERS

32. *n.* Electrical current.
Before WW2 acceptable symbols for current had been C for obvious reasons, and sometimes A for amperage. After the war the Electrotechnical Commission was set up to standardise the symbols used in Electronics. . . . They decided that current would be called I. The reason is that in French current is known as "intensité de courant." —Phil Picton

33. *n.* (mathematics) Imaginary number (equal to the square root of -1).

i for the imaginary unit was first used by Leonhard Euler (1707–1783) in a memoir presented in 1777 but not published until 1794 in his "Institutionum calculi integralis." —Jeff Miller, "Earliest Uses of Various Mathematical Symbols"

34. *n.* (astronomy) The inclination of an orbit to the ecliptic.

35. *n.* (chemistry) The symbol for the element iodine in the periodic table.

36. *n.* (logic) The notation of a particular affirmative statement, such as "some humans are men." In categorical logic, the square of opposition describes the relationship between the universal affirmative *A*, the universal negative *E*, the particular affirmative *I*, and the particular negative *O*.

37. *n.* A unit vector parallel to the x-axis.

38. *n.* Candlepower.

The term candlepower is based on a measurement of the light produced by a pure spermaceti candle weighing one sixth of a pound, burning at a rate of 120 grams per hour. Spermaceti is found in the head of Sperm Whales, and once was used to make candles. —Bob Sherman, Candle History

FOREIGN MEANINGS

39. *interj.* (German) "What next?!"

40. *interj.* (German) "Nonsense! rubbish!"

41. *interj.* (German) "Certainly not!"

42. *conj.* (Polish) also, too.

FACTS AND FIGURES

43. Lowercase *i* earned the right to a dot owing to its small size. However, the Turkish capital *I* is sometimes dotted.

44. Most of Emily Dickinson's poems (over 150 of them) begin with the word *I.* For example, "I heard a Fly Buzz When I Died."

45. *American Health* has reported that the less one uses the first-person pronoun, the less one's risk of coronary heart disease.

J IN PRINT AND PROVERB

1. **(in literature)** *"They decided to substitute for the lost jack a piece of card-sized paper on which they were going to draw a face both ways up, a club, a capital J, and even the jack's name."* —Georges Perec, *Life: A User's Manual*

2. **(in literature)** *"J is the plowshare and the horn of plenty."* —Victor Hugo, quoted in *ABZ* by Mel Gooding

3. *n.* A written representation of the letter.

4. *n.* A device, such as a printer's type, for reproducing the letter.
   If my mind orders my right forefinger to type the letter J, it obeys. —Houston Smith, *Why Religion Matters: The Fate of the Human Spirit in an Age of Disbelief*

SHAPES AND DESIGNATIONS

5. *n.* Something having the shape of a J.
   [Puzzle] pieces shaped like J, K, L, M, W, Z, X, Y, and T. —Georges Perec, *Life: A User's Manual*

6. *n.* Something arbitrarily designated J (e.g., a person, place, or other thing).
   After J, there would be K and L and M, right down the alphabet. It's no use being sentimentally cynical about this, or cynically sentimental. Because J isn't really what I want. J has only the value of being now. J will pass, the need will remain. The need to get back into the dark, into the bed, into the warm naked embrace, where J is no more J than K, L, or M. —Christopher Isherwood, *Prater Violet*

7. *n.* J turn: "a test of a car's reliability, made by making a sudden sharp turn around an obstacle like
another car or an animal, resulting in a path that
looks something like a J." —Dr. John Burkardt
*As the first two attackers stormed out of the house
after them, Liz gunned the engine and screeched
the Jeep in a sharp J-turn, fishtailing until her tires
gripped the cobblestones and the vehicle straight-
ened out.* —Gail Lynds, *The Coil: A Novel*

8. *n.* Someone called J.
*[W]ho is sitting out on a curbing on Haight Street
but J—of Pump House days gone by.* —Tom Wolfe,
The Electric Kool-Aid Acid Test

9. *n.* J bar: a reinforcing rod whose cross-section is
J-shaped.

10. *n.* J stroke: in rowing, an oar or paddle stroke tra-
versing the figure of a J.
*I could see the outline of a kneeling man, drawing
the paddle through the water in silent J-strokes.*
—James Lee Burke, *Purple Cane Road*

11. *n.* J bolt: a bolt in the shape of the letter J.

12. *n.* J box: "a J-shaped box through which fabric is
passed for a process such as bleaching." —Dr. John
Burkardt

PICK A NUMBER

13. *n.* A medieval Roman numeral for one. (See *I.*)

14. *n.* The tenth in a series, or the ninth (when I is omitted).
Toqueville did not include the letter J in numbering

J

his appendices. —Editor's footnote in *Democracy in America* by Alexis de Tocqueville

15. *n.* (economics) J curve: "a curve, suggestive of the shape of a J, that illustrates how after a currency falls in value, the trade deficit grows first before shrinking. It can also look like a reversed J, similar to a hyperbola, and is referred to in biology as representing a typical distribution of species in an area, with a few numerous species, and many species with just a few representatives." —Dr. John Burkardt

THE HEAT IS ON

16. *n.* (radiometry) Radiant intensity, or the flux from a point on a light source that is radiated into a unit solid angle.

17. *n.* (thermodynamics) Mechanical equivalent of heat, which is the energy of motion tied up in the ceaseless motion of the atoms in all substances.

MISCELLANEOUS

18. *n.* Any spoken sound represented by the letter.
The sound vibration of the consonant J means "sight, seeing, vision." —Joseph E. Rael, *Tracks of Dancing Light: A Native American Approach to Understanding Your Name*

19. *n.* The tenth letter of the alphabet.
He checked the mechanism. He stooped and typed C. The letter J lit up. He typed L and got a U. A, I, R and E yielded, successively, X, P, Q, and Q again. —Robert Harris, referring to the infamous Nazi Enigma code in his novel *Enigma*

20. *n.* The tenth section in a piece of music.

21. *n.* J bag: a golf bag used for carrying clubs.

22. *n.* J stik: a joystick used in video game machines which allows for fast motions.

FOREIGN MEANINGS
23. *n.* (French) Zero, as in *le jour J,* "zero day."

FACTS AND FIGURES
24. In Medieval Latin, the letter *J* developed as a form of *I,* and both were used interchangeably. Under the influence of French, *J* became a separate sign with its own phonetic value.

K IN PRINT AND PROVERB

1. **(in literature)** The protagonist in Franz Kafka's works *The Trial* and *The Castle*.

2. **(in literature)** Prince K is Razumov's mysterious benefactor (and unacknowledged father) in Joseph Conrad's *Under Western Eyes*.

3. **(in literature)** Author David James Duncan offers a list of his own definitions for K in his novel *The Brothers K*:

   2. to fail, to flunk, to fuck up, to fizzle, or 3. to fall short, fall apart, fall flat, fall by the wayside, or on deaf ears, or hand times, or into disrepute or disrepair, or 4. to come unglued, come to grief, come to blows, come to nothing, or 5. go to the dogs, go through the roof, go home in a casket, go to hell in a hand basket, or 6. to blow your cover, blow your chances, blow your cool, blow your stack, shoot your wad, bitch the deal, buy the farm, bite the dust, only 7. to recollect an oddball notion you first heard as a crimeless and un-K'ed child but found so nonsensically paradoxical that you had to ignore it or defy it or betray it for decades before you could begin to believe that it might possibly be true, which is that 8. to lose your money, your virginity, your teeth, health or hair, 9. to lose your home, your innocence, your balance, your friends, 10. to lose your happiness, your hopes, your leisure, your looks, and yea, even your memories, your vision, your mind, your way, 11. in short (and as Jesus K. Rist once so uncompromisingly put it) to lose your very self, 12. for the sake of another, is 13. sweet irony, the only way you're ever going to save it. —David James Duncan, The Brothers K

4. **(in literature)** A misplaced letter of foreboding in Cathleen Schine's *Love Letter*:

   Johnny spun to face a bookcase of art criticism and wondered desperately if K came before or after

N. The alphabet, a pillar, a solace and a certainty since kindergarten, had suddenly deserted him. He stood, bewildered and staring, as if he'd suffered a crisis of faith. Does the alphabet exist? If the alphabet exists, why is there so much suffering in the world? The alphabet is dead.

5. (in film) The name of an atoll that shipwrecks the comedians Laurel and Hardy in the 1951 film *Atoll K.*

6. (in literature) "K" is the title of a poem by Erin Belieu, anthologized in the 2000 book *One Above and One Below: New Poems.*

7. (in literature) *"K is the angle of reflection equal to the angle of incidence, a key to geometry."* —Victor Hugo, quoted in *ABZ* by Mel Gooding

8. *n.* A written representation of the letter.
Look at the kinks in those k's. —William H. Gass, *The Tunnel*
The Chinese cyborg took the chips in the center of the table, sorted through them and found one marked with a K. —Pat Cadigan, *Dervish Is Digital*

9. *n.* A device for reproducing the letter.

10. *n.* The color black, as in the acronym CMYK (cyan, magenta, yellow, and black).
The letter K is used to designate black because the B is already in use for the color blue. —Taz Tally, *SilverFast: The Official Guide*

SCIENCE AND TECHNOLOGY

11. *n.* In computer technology, the number 1,024, as in a computer with 32K of memory.

12. *n.* Carat, a measure of precious metals such as gold. *Gold in its pure state would be 24 carat. Here, a carat is a measure of the fineness or purity, and must not be confused with the carat weight of gemstones, which is one-fifth of a gram. So while 24K gold is 100 per cent, 18K gold would be 18 parts gold and 6 parts of another metal or alloy.* —Express India

13. *n.* A unit vector parallel to the z-axis.

14. *n.* Boltzmann's constant, which relates changes in the energy for individual molecules in an ideal gas to changes in temperature.

15. *n.* Dissociation constant, or the equilibrium constant for the dissociation of an acid into a hydrogen ion and an anion.

16. *n.* Ionization constant, or the equilibrium constant for the hydrolysis reaction associated with a base.

17. *n.* A vitamin (from alfalfa).
Vitamin K is a blood clotting agent; it works in the liver to form the substances that promote normal blood clotting. Because vitamin K is also manufactured in the body by intestinal bacteria, as well as being available in many foods, deficiency is uncommon in healthy adults. [Deficiency] may develop as a result of taking antibiotics, which destroy the normal intestinal bacteria. People with malabsorption disorders, some liver diseases, and chronic diarrhea are susceptible to vitamin K deficiency. Because breast milk contains little vitamin K and newborns do not have the intestinal bacteria to produce their own, vitamin K supplements may be given at birth. Good sources of vitamin K include dark green leafy vegetables, eggs, cheese, pork, and liver. —American Medical Association

18. *n.* **(chemistry)** The symbol for the element potassium in the periodic table.

19. *n.* **(biology)** Lysine, an amino acid.

20. *n.* **(geology)** The Cretaceous period.
    Geologists use the letter K to symbolize the Cretaceous, from the equivalent German word "Kreide" (chalk).
    —Walter Alvarez, *T. Rex and the Crater of Doom*

21. *n.* **(astronomy)** A class of stars in between yellow and red.

BALLS AND BOULDERS

22. *n.* In baseball, a strikeout.

23. *n.* A mountain, as in K 2 (the second highest mountain on earth, located in the Karakoram range in Pakistan).

SHAPES AND DESIGNS

24. *n.* Something having the shape of a K.
    [The three crossing roads] looked like a capital letter K, lightly peppered with habitation where the three lines of the letter met. —Lee Child, *Without Fail*
    Dad's modest party had been overrun by . . . the deformed, whose legs looked like the letter K. —Ben Okri, *The Famished Road*
    Colette was so excited that before she could stop herself, she twisted her body until it resembled the letter K and the letter S at the same time. —Lemony Snicket, *The Carnivorous Carnival* (A Series of Unfortunate Events, Book 9)

25. *n.* K truss: "a building truss with a vertical member and two obliques, which forms a K."
—Dr. John Burkardt

26. *n.* Something arbitrarily designated K (e.g., a person, place, or other thing).

27. *n.* A 1986 Chrysler limousine, also called the K-Car. *We watched stupidly as they crossed between two parked cars and slid into the backseat of a black K-car that had rolled up from behind us in the street, then immediately took off.* —Jonathan Lethem, *Motherless Brooklyn*

NUMBERS

28. *n.* The eleventh in a series.

29. *n.* A Roman numeral for 250.

30. *n.* (calculus) Index of summation. *[T]he letter K is called the index of summation. [However,] It is not essential to use k as the index of summation.* —Howard A. Anton, *Calculus, Early Transcendentals Combined*

WARDS AND WEAPONS

31. *n.* K Block: a ward in a building set aside for very high security or for the temporarily insane. *K Block is guarded 24 hours a day, and response measures are in place in case of a terrorist incursion. Specifics on security are classified, though it's almost certain that military personnel from other nearby installations would be part of an antiterrorist response. Suffice [it] to say, said [Don*

Smythe, director of chemical operations at the U.S. Army's Umatilla Chemical Depot in Hermiston, Oregon], that intruders "might be able to get in, but they definitely wouldn't be able to get out."
—Alex Tizon, *The Seattle Times*

32. *n.* K-bar: a fairly large, heavy-duty survival knife with a serrated top edge used by the U.S. Marine Corps. According to tradition, when a Marine ends his tour of duty, he gives his K-bar to his best friend.
   I reached into a desk drawer and pulled out a dangerous-looking K-Bar Bowie knife, which I proceeded to wave menacingly in the air. It was almost 14 inches long, painted dull black and weighing about nine pounds. Any bozo could easily use it to crack open a coconut with one blunt and inarticulate blow. "Government issue," I said. "Cuts through a human limb like a Ginsu through a ripe tomato. Here, strap this on in case things get crazy."
   —Kyle Bradley Cassidy, "The True Story of the Gypsy's Wedding"

33. *n.* A military code used on D-Day.
   Two ten-man groups were to mark that area with lights, each one flashing up into the night sky the code letter K. —Cornelius Ryan, *The Longest Day: The Classic Epic of D-Day*

34. *n.* K gun: a compact antisubmarine weapon which propels depth charges from a battleship. It replaced the Y gun on American ships in 1942.

MISCELLANEOUS

35. *n.* The eleventh letter of the alphabet.
   It is a killer—knowledge is—the big K. —William H. Gass, *The Tunnel*

The letter K has been a favorite with me—it seemed a strong, incisive sort of letter. —George Eastman, on how he coined the name Kodak, quoted in *The New Positioning: The Latest on the World's #1 Business Strategy*, by Jack Trout

36. *n.* Any spoken sound represented by *K*.
Pemulis's snort sounds like the letter K. —David Foster Wallace, *Infinite Jest*
The sound vibration of the consonant K means "planting, planting field, sowing." —Joseph E. Rael, *Tracks of Dancing Light: A Native American Approach to Understanding Your Name*

37. *n.* The eleventh section in a piece of music.

38. *n.* A symbol in a Treasury note.
The letter k indicates that non-U.S. citizens are exempt from withholding. —Michael Constas, *The International Investment Sourcebook*

39. *n.* K-rations: food provided to soldiers during combat.
K rations were far more common [than C rations], if for no other reasons than they weighed less and were easier to carry.... Lathrop Mitchell, a medic in the 92nd Infantry Division in Italy, described K rations in his diary: "These K rations come in a waxed box like a small cigar box. The food consists of a can of cheese or Spam, crackers, meat loaf in a can, instant coffee, candy, cigarettes, gum and toilet paper."
—John C. McManus, *The Deadly Brotherhood*

FACTS AND FIGURES

40. The ancient Romans branded false accusers with a K.

L IN PRINT AND PROVERB

1. **(phrase)** An "L-shaped bottom" is "what happens when the stock market drops sharply and doesn't come back up for a long, long time." —Dr. John Burkardt

2. **(in literature)** *"The preyful Princess pierc'd and prick'd a pretty pleasing pricket; Some say a sore, but not a sore, till now made sore with shooting. The dogs did yell: put L to sore, then sorel jumps from thicket, or pricket sore, or else sorel; the people fall a-hooting. If sore be sore, then L to sore makes fifty sores o'sorel: Of one sore I an hundred make by adding but one more L."* —William Shakespeare, *Love's Labor's Lost*, IV.ii.56–61. Wordplay here involves *sorel*, a deer of the third year; *sore*, a deer of the fourth year; *L*, the Roman numeral fifty.

3. **(in literature)** *"She gazed at me with vacant, drunken composure, standing colt-like on the outer edge of her black-stockinged foot so the ankle was twisted inward in a startling, effortless L."* —Donna Tartt, *The Secret History*

4. **(in literature)** *"Long lines of women, bent double like inverted capital Ls, work their way slowly across the fields."* —George Orwell, "Marrakech"

5. **(in literature)** *"L is the leg and the foot."* —Victor Hugo, quoted in *ABZ* by Mel Gooding

6. *n.* A written representation of the letter.

7. *n.* A device, such as a printer's type, for reproducing the letter.

BY RAIL

8. *n.* An elevated railroad, such as the one in Chicago, Illinois.

The friction of steel wheel flanges grinding against tracks can produce the distinctive ear-piercing screech of an elevated train. It's been 100 years since Chicago's "L" made its first circuit of the Loop.... Today, more than 436,000 people ride the "L" every weekday. —The Chicago Tribune

Have I still not made my peace with the afternoons of youth when I fled Reality, via the Third Avenue "L," to get to my little womb off third base at the Polo Grounds? —J. D. Salinger, *Seymour: An Introduction*

ANGULARITY

9. *n.* A right angle.

10. *n.* An extension of a house or building that gives the whole an L shape.
    An L of the house where she was born is still standing. —Harper's Weekly
    It was L-shaped and there was a small window high in one of the walls. Light spilled from it in a theatrical beam illuminating whatever was contained in the foot of the L. —Jeremy Dyson, *Never Trust a Rabbit*

11. *n.* Something having the shape of an L.
    Separated from the main part of the studio by an L-shaped piece of furniture. —Georges Perec, *Life: A User's Manual*
    The place was almost dark even in the middle of a sunny day: a narrow, long, L-shaped room with only one entrance, dim light laboring through its two window-panes, enough to find your way to a table; otherwise, electric mock-candles cast a weak glow on each table, hardly enough to read the menu. —Reza Ordoubadian, "The Body Who Invaded My Life"
    It must be explained here that my cabin had the form of the capital letter L, the door being within the

angle and opening into the short part of the letter.
—Joseph Conrad, *The Secret Sharer*

12. *n.* L bar: a steel beam whose cross-section is L-shaped.

13. *n.* L block: an L-shaped concrete building block.

14. *n.* L pipe: a section of pipe bent at a 90-degree angle.

15. *n.* L square: a carpenter's ruler which is L-shaped.

16. *n.* L sill: in carpentry, "a sill used in a building frame. A plate is attached to a basement wall, and an upright header is fixed to the outer edge of the plate, forming an L." —Dr. John Burkardt

SCIENTIFIC MATTERS

17. *n.* (electronics) Inductance, or the quantity involved in the production of an electromotive force in a conductor by means of variations in the current. Inductance is essentially equivalent to inertia (or mass in the context of three-dimensional space).

18. *n.* Kinetic potential. Also called the "Lagrangian" (after Joseph Lagrange), the kinetic potential of a system is the quantity obtained by subtracting the system's potential energy from its kinetic energy.

19. *n.* (mathematics) In linear algebra, a matrix in which only zeros appear above the diagonal. *L is a lower triangular matrix.* —Marie A. Vitulli, "A Brief History of Linear Algebra and Matrix Theory"

20. *n.* (mechanics) L head: a gasoline engine commonly known as a flat-head motor, typical in automobiles manufactured before World War II.

NUMERIC EQUIVALENTS

21. *n.* In the U.K., a pound sterling.

22. *n.* A Roman numeral for 50.

23. *n.* The twelfth in a series.

24. *n.* (economics) Money demand.
     *The letter L is used to denote money demand
     because money is the economy's most liquid asset.*
     —N. Gregory Mankiw, *Macroeconomics*

MISCELLANEOUS

25. *n.* Any spoken sound represented by the letter.
     *The sound vibration of the consonant L means "ascending
     light."*—Joseph E. Rael, *Tracks of Dancing Light: A Native
     American Approach to Understanding Your Name*
     *For my nymphet I needed a diminutive with a lyri-
     cal lilt to it. One of the most limpid and luminous
     letters is "L." The suffix "-ita" has a lot of Latin
     tenderness, and this I required too. Hence: Lolita.
     However, it should not be pronounced as . . . most
     Americans pronounce it: Low-lee-ta, with a heavy,
     clammy "L" and a long "O." No, the first syllable
     should be as in "lollipop," the "L" liquid and delicate.*
     —Vladimir Nabokov, *The Annotated Lolita*
     *The password always contained the letter L, which
     the Japanese had difficulty pronouncing the way an
     American would.* —Eugene B. Sledge, *With the Old
     Breed: At Peleliu and Okinawa*

26. *n.* The twelfth letter of the alphabet.
     *Then, no doubt, the "l" had been dropped or had
     been replaced by an "h."* —Georges Perec, *Life:
     A User's Manual*
     [A]n Allied fighter plane with a yellow flag on its

*cockpit bearing the letter L had circled over Don
Calò's town; and inside a packet dropped by the
pilot—which fell near the town church and was
delivered by a villager to the home of Don Calò—
was a smaller replica of this yellow L flag.*
—Gay Talese, *Unto the Sons*

27. *n.* The twelfth section in a piece of music.
*Its final climactic statement at letter L ... comes as
something of a surprise, as the twelve previous ver-
sions of this figure, for all their variety of harmoni-
zation and orchestration, convey a consistency of
expression.* —Timothy L. Jackson, *Sibelius Studies*

28. *n.* Something arbitrarily designated L (e.g., a person,
place, or other thing).

29. *n.* Hell, in transliterations of the English Cockney
dialect, which drops the h-sound from the word.

30. *n.* An ancient sign indicating the geometric shape
of the square according to Herman R. Bangerter,
"Significance of Ancient, Geometric Symbols."

31. *n.* A source of material included in the New Testament.
*When we examine the corpus of Luke, we quickly
become aware that there is a significant amount of
uniquely Lucan material that appears nowhere else
in any gospel. New Testament scholars tend to call
this the L source. In the past it was asserted that L
represented the material available to Luke other
than Mark or Q. Lately, the suggestion has been
offered that Luke was himself the creative genius
who wrote the L material and that his only external
primary sources were Mark and Matthew.* —John
Shelby Spong, *Liberating the Gospels: Reading the
Bible with Jewish Eyes*

M IN PRINT AND PROVERB

1. (phrase) *To have an M under one's girdle* means to show courtesy by using the title Mr., Mrs., or Miss.

2. (in literature) *"The letter m in the word am means I; so that in the expression I am, a superfluous and useless rudiment has been retained."* —Charles Darwin, *The Descent of Man*

3. (in literature) *"M is a mountain or a camp with tents pitched in pairs."* —Victor Hugo, quoted in *ABZ* by Mel Gooding

4. *n.* In printing, a pica or unit of measure ("em" space).

5. *n.* A written representation of the letter. *Through one street and the next, until she'd come upon the red M of a Metro station. Descending, she'd purchased, with too large a bill and some difficulty, tokens of what appeared to be luminous plastic, the color of glow-in-the-dark toy skeletons, each with its own iconic M.* —William Gibson, *Pattern Recognition* *[The curve of the handwritten line,] galloping like the wind, cutting across itself, soars up to the sky, so that it can start turning into the letter M.* —Peter Esterhazy, *Celestial Harmonies: A Novel*

6. *n.* A device, such as a printer's type, for reproducing the letter.

CLASSIFICATIONS AND DESIGNATIONS

7. *n.* Classification of a rifle, as in M-1 and M-16. *Do you wonder why that rifle/Is hanging in my den?/You know I rarely take it down/But I touch it now and then./It's rather slow and heavy/By standards of today/But not too many years ago/It swept*

the rest away./It's held its own in battles/Through snow, or rain, or sun/And I had one just like it,/This treasured old M-1. —R. A. Gannon, "M-1"

8. *n.* Something arbitrarily designated M (e.g., a person, place, or other thing).
[*In response to a blind taste test conducted by Pepsi, in which people were asked to choose between two products labeled Q and M, the Coca-Cola Company] churned out a bewildering set of statements and commercials aimed at disparaging Pepsi's results, starting with the claim that people had a psychological preference for the letter M over the letter Q, unfairly skewing the outcome [in Pepsi's favor]. Pepsi . . . hit back immediately with a new set of taste tests using the letters L and S that also detected a preference for Pepsi. Coca-Cola answered that salvo with a faux-comic spot in which people explained why they liked the letter L better than the letter S.* —Frederick L. Allen, *Secret Formula*

9. *n.* Someone called M.
[*I am psychically picking up on] the letter M. It's very strong in this room. . . . You have helped me before; I need your help now, M. M, come to me. I will aid you in your fight against the spirit you oppose. But you must tell me where to look. Are you trying to reach me, M?* —*Dark Shadows*, Episode 648
Yet Leonardo must have hoped that . . . some objective observer would one day seize on the image of this mysterious woman linked with the letter "M" and ask the obvious questions. Who was this "M" and why was she so important? —Lynn Picknett, *The Templar Revelation: Secret Guardians of the True Identity of Christ*

10. *n.* The thirteenth in a series.

11. *n.* The Millennium Hotel in Minneapolis, Minnesota.
The M has several spaces for comfy socializing.
—Davey Snyder, quoted in NeilGaiman.com

HEALTH ISSUES

12. *n.* An antigen of human blood responsible for the
production of antibodies.
*The M antigen, and its antithetical partner, N,
were first detected using sera obtained from
rabbits immunized with human red cells.*
—Immucor

13. *n.* A vitamin (folic acid).
*Folic acid is essential to many of the body's enzyme
activities, including the synthesis of protein and
the genetic materials RNA and DNA. It also works
with vitamin B12 to produce red blood cells. Folic
acid may help prevent some cancers, heart disease,
and stroke. Adequate intake during pregnancy is
crucial, as folic acid appears to protect against
some birth defects. . . . Rich sources of folic acid
include vegetables (particularly the dark-green
ones); organ meats, whole-wheat products, legumes,
and mushrooms.* —American Medical Association

SCIENTIFIC MATTERS

14. *n.* A Roman numeral for 1,000.

15. *n.* With a line above it, a Roman numeral for
1,000,000.

16. *n.* A computer programming language.
*M is a procedural, general purpose language with
well-developed database handling capabilities. . . .*

*[It has been theorized that] the choice of a single
letter [name] was to get a free ride from the popu-
larity of C, a single letter compiler which is very
popular.* —Chris Bonnici

17. *n.* **(calculus)** The lower limit of summation.

18. *n.* **(astronomy)** A class of red stars.
[F]or red stars like Betelgeuse, we use the letter M.
—Dennis Richard Danielson, *The Book of the Cosmos*

CONTRACTION 'M

19. *v.* Am. *I'm going.*

20. *pronoun.* Him. *Give 'm the whole story.*

21. *n.* Madam. *Yes 'm.*

MISCELLANEOUS

22. *n.* Any spoken sound represented by the letter.
*The sound vibration of the consonant M means
"to bring forth, manifesting, matter."* —Joseph E.
Rael, *Tracks of Dancing Light: A Native American
Approach to Understanding Your Name*

23. *n.* The thirteenth letter of the alphabet.
*"They drew all manner of things—everything that
begins with an M."
"Why with an M?" said Alice.
"Why not?" said the March Hare.* —Lewis Carroll,
Alice in Wonderland
Big guy, looks . . . what's the word. Begins with an M.
—Neil Gaiman, *American Gods*
Two massive columns supported a lintel that dipped

*in the center to a sharp point, giving the whole
monument the shape of a gigantic letter "M."* —Stan
McDaniel, *The Letterseeker*
*[K]illing some hours by circling in blue ball-point
ink every uppercase M in the front section of a
month-old* New York Times. —Jonathan Franzen,
The Corrections

24. *n.* Something having the shape of an M.
*Breakfast time is his time for sitting atop that
spherical white buoy . . . his wings held in the shape
of an M.* —William Calvin, *The Cerebral Symphony*
*The slope was so sheer it hid the M-stone as if it had
never existed, and the glare from the sun flashed off
the wet surface like a mirror.* —Stan McDaniel,
The Letterseeker
*Both orbital rims and brow ridges are oblique in
such a way as to describe a stretched-out letter
M above the eyes.* —Stephen Rogers Peck, *Atlas of
Human Anatomy for the Artist*

25. *n.* The thirteenth section in a piece of music.

26. *n.* M roof: a double-peaked roof.

27. *n.* Deep dreamless sleep.
*M [of the sacred Hindu syllable AUM] is of Deep
Dreamless Sleep, where (as we say) we have "lost"
consciousness, and the mind (as described in the
Indian texts) is "an undifferentiated mass or con-
tinuum of consciousness unqualified," lost in darkness.* —Joseph Campbell, *The Mythic Image*

M

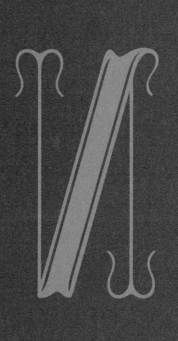

N IN PRINT AND PROVERB

1. *conj.* (informal, sometimes without apostrophe)
And. *Shop 'n Save*
At the corner, he stopped to look in the window of
Bric'n'Brac, a junk shop with sad pretensions. —Val
McDermid, *Wire in the Blood*

2. *n.* In printing, an "en" unit of measure, half the
width of an "em."

3. *n.* A written representation of the letter.
His capital N and the loop of his g swooped like
kite's tails. His t was a dagger thrusting down.
—Poppy Brite, *Lost Souls*
On this occasion, FOUAYANG was written as a
single word. One A is canted to the left and one to
the right, the Y looks like an X, and the legs of the
N undulate gracefully, like a child's drawing of a
wave. —Anne Fadiman, *The Spirit Catches You and*
You Fall Down

4. *n.* A device, such as a printer's type, for reproducing the letter.

5. *n.* A winner of the Nobel Prize.
One of the N crowd. —István Hargittai, *The Sydney*
Morning Herald, December 6, 2003.

6. (in literature) *"N is a gate with a diagonal bar."*
—Victor Hugo, quoted in *ABZ* by Mel Gooding

NUMBERS

7. *n.* (mathematics) an indefinite whole number, as
in the "nth degree."
I am a man to the nth degree, I swear it. —Thomas
Mann, *The Magic Mountain*

*Then we deploy that new technique to the nth
degree, putting to it every possible question that
might apply or be of further research value, until
we've exhausted the possibilities. —Candice Pert,
Molecules of Emotion: The Science Behind Mind-
Body Medicine*

8. *n.* An infinite number countable only by the godhead.
   *Man owns three or twenty, or however far he
   can count, and then comes the archetype of the N
   and that is in the hands of a godhead.*
   —Marie-Louise von Franz, *On Divination and
   Synchronicity*

9. *n.* The fourteenth in a series.

10. *n.* A Roman numeral for 90.

11. *n.* (calculus) The upper limit of summation.

MISCELLANEOUS

12. *n.* The fourteenth letter of the alphabet.
    *You are not allowed to ask why Swann has been
    spelled with two n's. —Quentin Crisp, How to Go to
    the Movies*
    *Ralph is phoning from "O" while Macy relaxes on
    "N." —Richard O'Brien and Jim Sharman, Shock
    Treatment*
    *Johnny spun to face a bookcase of art criticism and
    wondered desperately if K came before or after
    N. The alphabet, a pillar, a solace and a certainty
    since kindergarten, had suddenly deserted him. He
    stood, bewildered and staring, as if he'd suffered
    a crisis of faith. Does the alphabet exist? If the*

alphabet exists, why is there so much suffering in the world? The alphabet is dead. —Cathleen Schine, *The Love Letter*

He tried to skip n and go on, but n kept doggedly coming up in his mind, demanding an answer. —Kevin Kelly (referring to a game of listing, according to the alphabet, each chemical reaction bearing the discoverer's name), *Out of Control: The New Biology of Machines, Social Systems, and the Economic World*

13. *n.* Any spoken sound represented by the letter.
The sound vibration of the consonant N means "the personal and infinite self." —Joseph E. Rael, *Tracks of Dancing Light: A Native American Approach to Understanding Your Name*

14. *n.* Someone called N.
I have known very few prosperous men of letters; N— represents for me the best and brightest side of literary success. —George Gissing, *The Private Papers of Henry Ryecroft*

15. *n.* Something having the shape of an N.
We make "Noodle Ns" in my class. I have a volunteer cut out a cardboard lowercase n for each child. They glue noodles all over it. —Bridgewater [Massachusetts] Elementary School

16. *n.* Something arbitrarily designated N (e.g., a person, place, or other thing).
The character N, which Rees says "measures the strength of electrical forces that hold atoms together, divided by the force of gravity between them," is explained next to the description of a star and a black hole. —Thomas Harrell, Fox News

17. *n.* The fourteenth section in a piece of music.

18. *n.* The love of God.
    *[T]he letter N is for the key of his eternal, steadfast
    love.* —Willis Barnstone, "The Closing Psalm,"
    The Other Bible

SCIENTIFIC MATTERS

19. *n.* (biology) Asparagine, an amino acid.

20. *n.* (biology) An antigen of human blood respon-
    sible for the production of antibodies.
    *The M antigen, and its antithetical partner, N, were
    first detected using sera obtained from rabbits
    immunized with human red cells.* —Immucor

21. *n.* (chemistry) The symbol for the element nitrogen
    in the periodic table.

22. *n.* (chemistry) The Avogadro constant *N* equals
    the number of atoms or molecules contained in
    a mole, which is defined as a mass in grams equal
    to the atomic or molecular weight of a substance.

23. *n.* Index of refraction.

24. *n.* The neutralizing force in the cosmic property of
    a substance.
    *When a substance is the conductor of the third or
    neutralizing force, it is called "nitrogen," and, like
    the nitrogen of chemistry, it is designated by the
    letter N.* —P. D. Uspenskii, *In Search of the Miracu-
    lous: Fragments of an Unknown Teaching*

N

CONTRACTION 'N

25. *contraction.* In. *Where* 'n *the heck is he?*

26. *contraction.* Than. *It's hotter* 'n *blazes outside.*

FOREIGN MEANINGS

27. *n.* (Spanish) An unknown person, as in *El Señor N.*

O IN PRINT AND PROVERB

1. (phrase) *Round as Giotto's O:* said of work that is flawless but done with little effort. Giotto was an Italian painter who could draw a perfect *O* freehand.

2. (phrase) *O per se:* the letter O by itself makes a word.

3. (in literature) As marks of smallpox: *"O that your face were not so full of O's."* —William Shakespeare, *Love's Labor's Lost,* V.ii.45

4. (in literature) As stars: *"All yon fiery Oes."* —William Shakespeare, *A Midsummer Night's Dream,* III.ii.188

5. (in literature) *"May we cram within this wooden O the very casques that did affright the air at Agincourt?"* —William Shakespeare, *Henry V,* Prologue, 13–15

6. (in literature) *"The little O, the earth."* —William Shakespeare, *Antony and Cleopatra,* V.ii.81

7. (in literature) As an affliction: *"Why should you fall into so deep an O?"* —William Shakespeare, *Romeo and Juliet,* III.iii.90

8. (in literature) *"O, supreme trumpet, full of strange harsh sounds, / Silences which are crossed by Worlds and by Angels— / O, Omega, violet ray of Her Eyes!"* —Arthur Rimbaud, "Vowels"

9. (in literature) *"O me no O's."* —Ben Jonson, *The Case Is Altered,* V.i.

10. (in literature) *"Like a full-acorned boar, a German one, cried O! and mounted."* —William Shakespeare, *Cymbeline,* II.v.17

O

11. (in literature) *OPQRS, Etc.* is a play concerning the liberation of Ottoville, where the only official color is orange, where the alphabet begins with the letter O, and all decisions are made by Otto the Official.

12. (in literature) *"O is the sun."*—Victor Hugo, quoted in *ABZ* by Mel Gooding

13. *n.* A song, as in the "O's of Advent" (the seven Advent Anthems sung on the days preceding Christmas Eve, each containing a separate invocation to Christ beginning with O).

14. *n.* A written representation of the letter.

15. *n.* A device, such as a printer's type, for reproducing the letter.

EXPRESSIONS

16. *interj.* Oh!

17. *interj.* Indeed!

18. *interj.* Used before a name in direct address, especially in solemn or poetic language.
Turn backward, O Time. —Elizabeth Akers Allen, "Rock Me to Sleep"

19. *interj.* An expression of pain.
o it hurts my chest hurts my shoulder o o o i want my momma. —Stephen King, *Carrie*

20. *interj.* An exclamation of surprise.
"O my dearie," the wife said from her bed with a surprise at once delighted and grieved, "how big he was!"—Albert Camus, *The Fall*

O

21. *interj.* An expression of annoyance.
    O bother! —William Horwood, *Toad Triumphant*

22. *interj.* An expression of longing.
    *"O that his left hand were under my head, and that
    his right hand embraced me!"* —Andy FitzGibbon,
    The Kiss of Intimacy: the Soul's Longing After God

23. *interj.* An exclamation of gladness.

24. *interj.* An expression introducing a wish.
    O for a life of sensations rather than of thoughts!
    —John Keats, quoted in *What Is History? And Other
    Essays* by Michael Joseph Oakeshott

25. *interj.* An exclamation of wonder.
    But o! But o!/How very blue/The sea is! —Clive
    Barker, *Abarat*

26. *interj.* An exclamation of fear.

27. *interj.* An interjection at the end of a ballad or
    song, as in "Bingo was his name, O."

28. *interj.* An expression of earnestness.
    *[Marlene] Dietrich began to sing, her voice full of lan-
    guid melancholy, worldliness, the sadness of knowl-
    edge, and the longing for love. "O," exclaimed Weber,
    "she is the incarnation of sex. She makes me melt."*
    —Louis De Bernieres, *Corelli's Mandolin: A Novel*

29. *interj.* An expression of reassurance.
    *O, come on, another [drink of liquor] won't do you
    any harm.* —James Joyce, *Dubliners*

0

ZERO AND UP

30. *n.* The numeral zero.
    *He picks up the receiver, drops in a quarter, and
    dials the "0" for Operator.* —David Lynch, *Mulhol-
    land Drive*

31. *n.* A cipher (mathematical symbol denoting
    absence of quantity).
    Thou art an O without a figure. —William Shake-
    speare, *King Lear*, I.iv.212

32. *n.* A medieval Roman numeral for 11.

33. *n.* The fifteenth in a series.

MISCELLANEOUS

34. *v.* Owe.
    *"I must say, I didn't know what to make of it when I
    saw your note." He meant the one I'd left him when
    he fell asleep on me in the conference room. It lay
    crinkled on the coffee table between us, a single
    sheet of yellow legal paper on which I'd scribbled
    three large letters: I O U. "Well, I did owe you. I
    owed you an apology and a kitten. Now you got
    both."* —Lisa Scottoline, *Legal Tender*

35. *n.* A complete, whole person.
    *You see, the problem with this completed person,
    this O, that both people think they have reached, is
    that it has taken two people to make this one whole
    person, one supplying the female energy and one
    supplying the male.* —James Redfield, *The Celestine
    Prophecy*

0

36. *n.* The fifteenth letter of the alphabet.
    *"His name," said the palmist, thoughtful looking, "is
    not spelled out by the lines, but they indicate 'tis a
    long one, and the letter 'o' should be in it. There's no
    more to tell."* —O. Henry, *41 Stories by O. Henry*

37. *n.* Any spoken sound represented by the letter.
    *The sound vibration of the vowel O means "inno-
    cence, childlike innocence, circle of light, hollow
    bone, hollow reed, medicine wheel."* —Joseph E.
    Rael, *Tracks of Dancing Light: A Native American
    Approach to Understanding Your Name*

38. *n.* (logic) The notation of a particular negative
    statement, such as "some humans are not
    men." In categorical logic, the square of opposi-
    tion describes the relationship between the uni-
    versal affirmative *A*, the universal negative *E*,
    the particular affirmative *I*, and the particular
    negative *O*.

39. *n.* Something arbitrarily designated O (e.g., a per-
    son, place, or other thing).
    You're sounding hale and fit, O. —David Foster Wal-
    lace, *Infinite Jest*

40. *n.* The stigma of an open relationship.
    *A giant O would hang above our house, a scarlet let-
    ter emblazoned upon the sky for the general protec-
    tion of the citizenry.* —Daniel Jones, *The Bastard
    on the Couch: 27 Men Try Really Hard to Explain
    Their Feelings About Love, Loss, Fatherhood, and
    Freedom*

41. *n.* Something having the shape of an O.
    In this old house we've misfitting screens. Tiny

0

*insects are dying of my lamps. . . . They write Os in
the air, perfect Os, as I was taught.* —William H.
Gass, *The Tunnel*

*The three fish bobbed up, pale-white silvered
ghost carp, staring at us, or seeming to, the O's of
their mouths continually opening and closing, as if
they were talking to us in some silent, secret language
of their own.* —Neil Gaiman, *Smoke and Mirrors*

42. *adj.* Oval in shape.
*His mouth opened in a wide O as he clutched his
groin with intent, slowly sank to his knees, and
doubled over until his forehead rested on the lawn.*
—George C. Chesbro, *The Language of Cannibals*

43. *n.* The fifteenth section in a piece of music.
*In the midst of the rehearsal [of the Rachmaninoff con-
certo, conductor Desiré] Defauw stopped the orchestra
and said: "Gentlemen, let us play again one bar before
letter O." When the bar had been played Defauw smiled
with pleasure and said: "Gentlemen, Mr. Horowitz says
I conduct that bar better than any conductor in the
world."* —Oscar Levant, *The Memoirs of an Amnesiac*

44. *prep.* In.

45. *n.* A rating of "morally offensive" according to the
U.S. Conference of Catholic Bishops Office for Film
and Broadcasting Classification.

SCIENTIFIC MATTERS

46. *n.* A blood type.
*Genes for types A and B are dominant, and will
always be expressed. Type O is recessive. A child who*

0

inherits one A and one O gene will be type A. Simi-
larly, a child who inherits one B and one O gene will
be type B. If both an A and a B gene are passed on, a
child will be type AB. Only a child who inherits one O
gene from each parent will be type O. —Mayo Clinic

47. *n.* A person with type O blood.
    Since Os have been blessed with such strong stom-
    ach acid and respective enzymes, they are able to
    metabolize almost everything, even those foods not
    recommended for them. —Steven M. Weissberg,
    MD, *InnerSelf Magazine*

48. *n.* (chemistry) The symbol for the element oxygen
    in the periodic table.
    "Think you could swim in heavy water?" "H two O
    two? Very buoyantly, I imagine." —Iain Banks, *The*
    Business

49. *n.* The passive force in the cosmic property of a
    substance.
    When a substance is the conductor of the second or
    the passive force, it is called "oxygen," and, like the
    oxygen of chemistry, it is designated by the letter O.
    —P. D. Uspenskii, *In Search of the Miraculous: Frag-*
    ments of an Unknown Teaching

50. *n.* (astronomy) A class of the bluest and hottest stars.

51. *n.* (medicine) O sign: the state of having one's mouth
    gaping open as in a mouth-breathing sleeping
    patient, a demented conscious patient, or a recently
    dead patient, coined by emergency room doctors.
    He's resting comfortably; positive O sign.
    —Sheilendr Khipple, "What's a Bed Plug? An LOL
    in NAD."

O

52. *n.* O horizon: the topmost layer of soil, consisting of decomposed organic matter.

CONTRACTION O'

53. *prep.* Of. *barrel* o' *fun*

54. of. O'*clock. will*-o'-*the-wisp*

55. Descendant of, as in the family name O'Reilly.

FOREIGN MEANINGS

56. *interj.* (Latin) Alas! *O tempora!* means "Alas! how times have changed for the worse."

57. *conj.* (Italian) Either, or, whether.

58. *prep.* (Polish) Of, for, at, by, about, against, with, to, over.

FACTS AND FIGURES

59. In Semitic, *O* is called "the eye."

60. To the Chinese Taoists, the circle represents the "Great Ultimate." It combines emptiness with fullness. It harmonizes the visible with the invisible.

61. Vowels are letters of the alphabet that are pronounced with an open or partially open mouth. *O* is the only vowel that forces you to imitate its shape with your mouth when you say it!

O

62. In Old English, *O* was called *oedel*, which means "home."

63. *O* is both a letter and the numeral zero. **As it is the additive identity, zero is necessary to our number system even though it has no value. Other letters which are also numbers include I, O, E, V, X, L, C, D, M, J, F, S, R, N, Y, T, H, K, B, G, P, Q, Z.**

0

P IN PRINT AND PROVERB

1. **(phrase)** William Oxberry (1784–1824) was called "the Five P's" because he was a publisher, printer, poet, publican, and player.

2. **(in literature)** *"After she left, I mused for a few seconds on what is called in the medical profession the 'p' phenomenon: the tendency of starched nurses' uniforms to make it seem as if all nurses were bountifully blessed in the bosom and this shaped like the letter 'p.' "* —Luke Rhinehart, *The Dice Man*

3. **(in literature)** *"I handed him two alphabet blocks and part of a half-eaten soda cracker. The howling ceased at once. He put the cracker in his mouth and banged the letter P against the plastic padding under him."* —Sue Grafton, *P Is for Peril*

4. **(in literature)** As a gentle letter of the alphabet: *"He remembers, as a child, poring over the word rape in newspaper reports, trying to puzzle out what exactly it meant, wondering what the letter p, usually so gentle, was doing in the middle of a word held in such horror that no one would utter it aloud."* —J. M. Coetzee, *Disgrace*

5. **(in literature)** As an antisocial letter of the alphabet: *"However, the letter P is much less friendly [than O and X]. It tends to lurk around just a few letters, and avoids 15 of them."* —Simon Singh, *The Code Book: The Science of Secrecy from Ancient Egypt to Quantum Cryptography*

6. **(in literature)** As the character of the bear in A.A. Milne's Winnie-the-Pooh stories: *" 'It's a Missage,' he said to himself, 'that's what it is. And that letter is a "P," and so is that, and so is that, and "P" means*

"Pooh," so it's a very important Message to me, and
I can't read it.' " —The Complete Tales & Poems of
Winnie-the-Pooh

7. (in literature) *"P is a porter with a load on his back."*
—Victor Hugo, quoted in *ABZ* by Mel Gooding

8. (in film) *Alphabet Pam* is a short 2004 film by Eva
Saks about a little girl who has a passion for the
letter P. The film was created for the *Sesame Street*
television program.

9. *n.* Behavior, as in the phrase "mind your p's and q's."
McQuade was too near his d t's *to be mindful of his*
p's *and* q's. —O. Henry, *The Fifth Wheel*

10. *n.* A written representation of the letter.
*There, cut in half, was a symbol—barely noticeable
because of the faded ink. But with the light from
Eugene's desk lamp behind it, it stood out clear as
day—the letter P with a lightning bolt running
through it.* —Marshall Younger, *Mysteries in Odyssey #1: Case of the Mysterious Message*
*Half-way up the hill on a prominent lump of grey
stone the size of a hayrick had been painted with
a large, lop-sided letter P in scarlet paint, so that
it was visible to any ship anchored in the lagoon.*
—Wilbur A. Smith, *Blue Horizon*

11. *n.* A device, such as a printer's type, for reproducing the letter.

12. *n.* Blind P: the editorial symbol for a paragraph, i.e., ¶.

MISCELLANEOUS

13. *n.* Any spoken sound represented by the letter.

*The sound vibration of the consonant P means
"heart, centre, sunset."* —Joseph E. Rael, *Tracks of
Dancing Light: A Native American Approach to
Understanding Your Name*

14. *n.* The sixteenth letter of the alphabet.
    *The letter P, that broad, provocative expanse
    between O and Q, is one of the most ambivalent of
    all the twenty-six, for in it one finds pleasure and
    pain, peace and pandemonium, prosperity and pov-
    erty.* —James Thurber, "The Watchers of the Night"
    *Another fortunate terminologist hit upon the word
    "psychical"—the p might be sounded or not, accord-
    ing to the taste and fancy of the pronouncer—and
    the fashionable children of a scientific age were
    thoroughly at ease.* —George Gissing, *The Private
    Papers of Henry Ryecroft*

15. *n.* The sixteenth in a series.

16. *n.* Something having the shape of a P.
    *Someone from the back would lean forward and say,
    "You guys, I need a rest stop." So then the driver
    would flash her lights and signal the other cars, and
    the entertainer would wave out the window and
    form her fingers into the shape of a P and every-
    body would get off at the next exit.* —Samantha
    Bennett, *Post-Gazette*
    *Thread the nylon through the left (inactive) ring,
    pulling the cord through with your left hand. Let
    the resulting loop hang freely. Notice that it drops
    naturally into the letter P.* —New Skete Monks, *The
    Art of Raising a Puppy*

17. *n.* A Roman numeral for 400.

18. *n.* Something arbitrarily designated P (e.g., a per-
    son, place, or other thing).

P

19. *n.* The sixteenth section in a piece of music.

20. *n.* A message-processing language.
P is a simple configuration language designed for specification of message processing instructions at application proxies. P can be used to instruct an intermediary how to manipulate the application message being proxied. —Alex Rousskov, "P: Message Processing Language."

21. *n.* P trap: a plumbing fixture with a P-shaped curl installed below a sink and acting as a water door to trap sewer gases.
"Was it clogged?" "I dropped something down it," she answered, digging around the P trap with her finger. —Karin Slaughter, *Blindsighted*

SCIENTIFIC MATTERS

22. *n.* A vitamin found in citrus and rose hips.
Vitamin P was first discovered in 1936 by Hungarian scientist Dr. Albert Szent-Gyorgyi, who found it within the white of the rind in citrus fruits. . . . The letter P, for permeability factor, was given to this group of nutrients because they improve the capillary linings' permeability and integrity— that is, the passage of oxygen, carbon dioxide, and nutrients through the capillary walls. —Elson M. Haas, MD, *Staying Healthy with Nutrition: The Complete Guide to Diet and Nutritional Medicine*

23. *n.* (chemistry) The symbol for the element phosphorous in the periodic table.

24. *n.* (logic) A symbol used to represent an arbitrary proposition.

P

P, q, and r were used as propositional letters by
Bertrand Russell in 1903 in The Principles of Math-
ematics. —Jeff Miller, "Earliest Uses of Various
Mathematical Symbols"

P

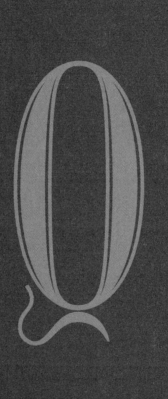

Q IN PRINT AND PROVERB

1. **(Biblical criticism)** Material common to the Gospels of Matthew and Luke that was not derived from the Gospel of Mark.

2. **(phrase)** *Q in a corner:* an old children's game.

3. **(phrase)** *In a merry Q:* to be in a good temper.

4. *n.* Behavior, as in "mind your p's and q's."

5. **(in literature)** As an evil letter: *"Evil Letter Q lacks the quintessential letter power: the ability to stand alone. While not lonely floating about in Iraq and Qatar, Q retains complete dependence on the otherwise mundane U, temptress vowel of the ages. Q, making the distinctive "KW" sound in nearly all walks of life—excluding, of course, ghetto, which retains little to no sense of phonetic logic—can logically be represented with two other letters, K and W, in that very order!"* —Eric Goulding

6. **(in literature)** As a high level of thought, reached via the near-genius ability to repeat every letter of the alphabet from A to Z accurately in order: *"It was a splendid mind. For if thought is like the keyboard of a piano, divided into so many notes, or like the alphabet is arranged in twenty-six letters all in order, then his splendid mind had no sort of difficulty in running over those letters one by one, firmly and accurately, until it had reached, say, the letter Q. He reached Q. Very few people in the whole of England ever reach Q. . . . But after Q? What comes next? After Q there are a number of letters the last of which is scarcely visible to mortal eyes, but glimmers red in the distance. Z is only reached once by one man in a generation. Still, if he could*

Q

*reach R it would be something. Here at least was Q.
He dug his heels in at Q. Q he was sure of. Q he could
demonstrate. If Q then is Q—R—Here he knocked
his pipe out, with two or three resonant taps on the
handle of the urn, and proceeded. 'Then R . . .' He
braced himself. He clenched himself.*" —Virginia
Woolf, *To the Lighthouse*

7. (in literature) As a letter that should be thrown
into a privet bush: *"He picked up the letter Q and
hurled it into a distant privet bush where it hit
a young rabbit. The rabbit hurtled off in terror
and didn't stop till it was set upon and eaten by a
fox which choked on one of its bones and died on
the bank of a stream which subsequently washed
it away. During the following weeks Ford Prefect
swallowed his pride and struck up a relationship
with a girl who had been a personnel officer on
Golgafrincham, and he was terribly upset when she
suddenly passed away as a result of drinking water
from a pool that had been polluted by the body of a
dead fox. The only moral it is possible to draw from
this story is that one should never throw the letter
Q into a privet bush, but unfortunately there are
times when it is unavoidable.* —Douglas Adams,
The Ultimate Hitchhiker's Guide to the Galaxy

8. (in literature) *"Q is a rump with a tail."* —Victor
Hugo, quoted in *ABZ* by Mel Gooding

9. *n.* A written representation of the letter.
*She had invented her own Q in kindergarten after
Miss Binney, the teacher, had told the class the letter
Q had a tail. Why stop there? Ramona had thought.*
—Beverly Cleary, *Ramona the Brave*, referring to a Q
drawn with ears and whiskers in addition to a tail.
*[I]t may be easier to make something of nothing than
nothing of something. Perceptual psychologist Ann*

Q

> *Treisman, of UC Berkeley, found that people shown a field of identical letter Q's with a simple O hidden in the middle did not see the O. The brain probably added the "tail" necessary to turn the O into a Q. And yet, people shown a field of O's had no problem finding a solitary Q. Finding the presence, in other words, was easy; but finding an absence was impossible for most people—even though the two situations were in all respects mirror images, entirely complementary.* —K. C. Cole, *The Hole in the Universe: How Scientists Peered over the Edge of Emptiness and Found Everything*

10. *n.* A device, such as a printer's type, for reproducing the letter.

11. *n.* An abbreviation for "cue," as written in play scripts to signal an actor to begin.

SEASICK

12. *n.* A boat, as in the armed Q-boat which is disguised as a fishing ship and used to decoy enemy submarines into gun range.

13. *n.* A fever like typhus, caused by a microorganism transmitted by raw milk or by ticks.

RATIOS AND AMOUNTS

14. *n.* (chiefly obsolete monetary unit) Half-a-farthing.

15. *n.* A medieval Roman numeral for 500.

16. *n.* The ratio of the reactance to the resistance of an oscillatory circuit.

17. *n.* The seventeenth in a series.

MISCELLANEOUS

18. *n.* Any spoken sound represented by the letter.
The sound vibration of the consonant Q means "initiation, eternal quest." —Joseph E. Rael, *Tracks of Dancing Light: A Native American Approach to Understanding Your Name*

19. *n.* The seventeenth letter of the alphabet.
Q is a letter we might very well spare in our Alphabet, if we would but use the serviceable K as he should be. —Ben Jonson, *Grammar*
The two of them had gone head-to-head for an hour now, and all he had left were the letters X and Q and there was nowhere on the Scrabble board to put them. —Susan Donovan, *Take a Chance on Me*

20. *n.* Something arbitrarily designated Q (e.g., a person, place, or other thing).
Books you were going to write with letters for titles. Have you read his F? O yes, but I prefer Q. Yes, but W is wonderful. O yes, W. —James Joyce, *Ulysses*

21. *n.* Something having the shape of a Q.
Generally, the stars that we can see look like a ball or maybe a disk. However, with high-resolving powerful telescopes like the Keck I in Hawaii, it may be possible to view more unusually-shaped stars deep in space. [The Wolf-Rayet 104 star] has a shape similar to the letter "Q." This Q-shaped star . . . is located in the direction of the Sagittarius asterism, about 4,800 light-years (1 light-year is approximately 5 trillion 900 billion miles or 9 trillion 460 billion kilometers) away from the Earth, and therefore looks like a vague image through common telescopes. —World Space News

Q

"Spare me, Oscar," she interjected, contorting herself into the letter Q. —Bill Richardson, *Waiting for Gertrude: A Graveyard Gothic*

22. *n.* The seventeenth section in a piece of music.
We can't work so much on detail we forget to put the whole passage in context. It's what I call the Letter Q Syndrome. We work so hard on letter Q, starting every rehearsal at that spot.... After the ninety-seventh time at Q, "Let's start at our favorite spot, letter Q." But the night of the concert, if we don't guard against this syndrome, where is the problem? It isn't letter Q; it is the few measures before Q. They know Q better than the back of their hands; they just don't know how to get Q in context. —Peter Loel, *Boonshaft, Teaching Music with Passion: Conducting, Rehearsing and Inspiring*
Against this background, the woodwind/brass motives (from letter Q) comprise three statements, sequential in pitch but also in time (since they involve a regular pulse), built to cumulative effect. —Timothy L. Jackson, *Sibelius Studies*

SCIENTIFIC MATTERS

23. *n.* (thermodynamics) Heat, or the energy flow from one object to another as a result of a temperature difference.

24. *n.* (biochemistry) The amino acid glutamine.
Glutamine is the most abundant amino acid (protein building block) in the body and is involved in more metabolic processes than any other amino acid. Glutamine is converted to glucose when more glucose is required by the body as an energy source. It serves as a source of fuel for cells lining the intestines. Without it, these cells waste away. It's

also used by white blood cells and is important for immune function. . . . Glutamine is found in many foods high in protein, such as fish, meat, beans, and dairy. —Mother Nature Health Encyclopedia

25. *n.* (in logic) a symbol used to represent an arbitrary proposition.
P, q, and r were used as propositional letters by Bertrand Russell in 1903 in The Principles of Mathematics. —Jeff Miller, "Earliest Uses of Various Mathematical Symbols"

26. *n.* (in mathematics) A matrix with special properties.
The Q is a matrix whose columns are orthonormal vectors. —Marie A. Vitulli, "A Brief History of Linear Algebra and Matrix Theory"

27. *n.* (medicine) Q sign: the state of having one's mouth open and tongue protruding, coined by emergency room doctors.
Looks like Mr. O'Reilly's not going to need his sleeping pills tonight—he's already got a positive Q sign showing. —Sheilendr Khipple, "What's a Bed Plug? An LOL in NAD"

Q

R IN PRINT AND PROVERB

1. **(in literature)** *"Nurse: Doth not rosemary and Romeo begin both with a letter? Romeo: Ay, nurse, what of that? Both with an R. Nurse: Ah, mocker, that's the dog's name."* —William Shakespeare, *Romeo and Juliet*, II.iv.206–209. In Shakespeare's time, R was called *littera canina*, "the dog's letter," because it sounded like a dog's growl.

2. **(in literature)** As a high level of thought, reached via the near-genius ability to repeat every letter of the alphabet from A to Z accurately in order: *"R is then—what is R? A shutter, like the leathern eyelid of a lizard, flickered over the intensity of his gaze and obscured the letter R. In that flash of darkness he heard people saying—he was a failure—that R was beyond him. He would never reach R. On to R, once more. R—."* —Virginia Woolf, *To the Lighthouse*

3. **(in literature)** *" 'Always fear the sun when there's an "r" in the month,' said Argyle. 'Always fear it "r" or no "r," I say. I'm frightened of it.' "* —D. H. Lawrence, *Aaron's Rod*

4. **(in literature)** *"The letter R was the last to go, it twisted in the flame, it curled outwards for a moment, becoming larger than ever. Then it crumpled too; the flame destroyed it. It was not ashes even, it was feathery dust."* —Daphne Du Maurier, *Rebecca*

5. **(in literature)** *"Sugar runs her gloved hands along the knots and curls [of a cast-iron fence]. It's only after a minute that she realises the dominant motif in the iron design is the letter 'R,' repeated hundreds and hundreds of times, hidden among the curlicues. 'Eureka,' she whispers. Adjusting her bonnet, she peers through the eye of the largest 'R'*

she can find."—Michel Faber, *The Crimson Petal and the White*

6. (in literature) *"R is the porter resting on his staff."* —Victor Hugo, quoted in *ABZ* by Mel Gooding

7. *v.* (informal) Are, as in "Oysters R in season" (because the oyster season occurs in months containing the letter R).

8. *n.* A written representation of the letter.
   An imitation-marble plaque . . . , now broken, . . . reads: CONSULTING R. —Georges Perec, *Life: A User's Manual*

9. *n.* A device, such as a printer's type, for reproducing the letter.

SCIENTIFIC MATTERS

10. *n.* Correlation coefficient.

11. *n.* Gas constant, as in the Ideal Gas Law equation $PV = nRT$.

12. *n.* An alkane molecule group.
    Alkyl groups are often represented by the letter R, just as halogens are often represented by the letter X. —Frank Pellegrini, *Organic Chemistry I*

13. *n.* (biology) Arginine, an amino acid.

14. *n.* (ecology) The Malthusian parameter, or the population growth rate per unit time in the Malthusian population growth model.

15. *n.* (logic) A symbol used to represent an arbitrary proposition.

R

P, q, and r were used as propositional letters by Bertrand Russell in 1903 in The Principles of Mathematics. —Jeff Miller, "Earliest Uses of Various Mathematical Symbols"

16. *n.* (mathematics) A matrix with special properties. *R is a square upper triangular invertible matrix with positive entries on its diagonal.* —Marie A. Vitulli, "A Brief History of Linear Algebra and Matrix Theory"

17. *n.* (astronomy) A "scale factor," which measures the distance between a chosen pair of galaxies and which increases as the universe expands. *When R doubles, the distance between every pair of galaxies doubles, and so on. Pushing the observed behaviour of the real Universe—its expansion—back to the point where everything was touching everything else, R starts out from zero, equivalent to the birth of the universe in an infinitely dense state.* —John R. Gribbin, *In Search of the Big Bang: The Life and Death of the Universe*

18. *n.* (organic chemistry) The chain of carbon atoms ("carbon skeleton") in an organic molecule. *The letter R represents the carbon skeleton of the molecule.* —Gerard J. Tortora, *Principles of Anatomy and Physiology*

19. *n.* R horizon: the layer of bedrock beneath the other soil layers.

MISCELLANEOUS

20. *n.* Any spoken sound represented by the letter. *"Ye'll observe," said Laird, academically, and rolling his r's . . .* —C.S. Forester, *Captain Horatio Hornblower* *The sound vibration of the consonant R means*

"radiance, radiating light, abundance." —Joseph E.
Rael, *Tracks of Dancing Light: A Native American
Approach to Understanding Your Name*

21. *n.* The eighteenth letter of the alphabet.
    *There was a big black mark on [the smokestack]
    that was a big R when you got close to it.* —John
    Kennedy Toole, *The Neon Bible*
    *A list of flavors, in appropriately colored chalks, was
    posted behind the counter. The R in Rainbow, I remem-
    ber, was written in peach.* —William H. Gass, *The Tunnel*

22. *n.* A subject in school, as in "the Three R's" (read-
    ing, writing, and arithmetic).
    *Johnston's early schooling grounded him well in the
    three R's and gave him a lifelong respect for learn-
    ing.* —Charles P. Roland, *Albert Sidney Johnston:
    Soldier of Three Republics*

23. *n.* A medieval Roman numeral for 80.

24. *n.* Something arbitrarily designated R (e.g., a per-
    son, place, or other thing).
    *Again R. chews wordlessly on his pipe, serene and
    satisfied.* —Luke Rhinehart, *The Dice Man*
    *[B]oth correlating epochs (temporal periods) were
    marked on the map with the same arbitrarily
    chosen symbol such as the letter R.* —Anatoly T.
    Fomenko, *History: Fiction or Science?*

25. *n.* The eighteenth in a series.

26. *n.* Something having the shape of an R.

27. *n.* The eighteenth section in a piece of music.

28. *n.* R color: "the addition of an R sound to a vowel."
    —Dr. John Burkardt

AT THE MOVIES

29. *adj.* A motion picture rating prohibiting admittance of anyone under seventeen years old not accompanied by a parent or guardian. **(See G, X.)** *[T]he R-rated brotherly chat for which he'd detoured through Seattle was in danger of being preempted by Everett's conflicting role in an eventually to be X-rated performance with the Sad Abdomen Lady!* —David James Duncan, *The Brothers K*

FACTS AND FIGURES

30. In England, an R was formerly used as a mark for rogues.

R

S IN PRINT AND PROVERB

1. **(phrase)** The Collar of S's, composed of a series of golden S's joined together, is a decoration restricted to the Lord Mayor of London.

2. **(in literature)** *S* is a 1988 novel by John Updike.

3. **(in literature)** Virginia Woolf wrote that S "is the serpent in the poet's Eden." —quoted in *The Alphabet Abecedarium* by Richard Firmage

4. **(in literature)** *"And it doesn't really matter, anyway, because we'll soon fatten him up again. All we'll have to do is give him a triple dosage of my wonderful Supervitamin Chocolate. Supervitamin Chocolate contains huge amounts of vitamin A and vitamin B. It also contains vitamin C, vitamin D, vitamin E, vitamin F, vitamin G, vitamin I, vitamin J, vitamin K, vitamin L, vitamin M, vitamin N, vitamin O, vitamin P, vitamin Q, vitamin R, vitamin T, vitamin U, vitamin V, vitamin W, vitamin X, vitamin Y, and, believe it or not, vitamin Z! The only two vitamins it doesn't have in it are vitamin S, because it makes you sick, and vitamin H, because it makes you grow horns on the top of your head, like a bull. But it does have a very small amount of the rarest and most magical vitamin of them all—vitamin Wonka."* —Roald Dahl, *Charlie and the Chocolate Factory*

5. **(in literature)** As an adjective that everybody knows and goes without saying: *"He is, as I see it and in my opinion, Amiable, Benevolent, Courteous, Dignified, Enamored, Firm, Gallant, Honorable, Illustrious, Loyal, Manly, Noble, Openhearted, Pleasing, Quick-witted, Rich, the Ss that everybody knows, and then Truthful, Valiant, X isn't included because it's a harsh letter, Y is the same I, and Z*

is Zealous in protecting your honor." —Miguel de Cervantes, *Don Quixote*

6. (in literature) *"S is a serpent."* —Victor Hugo, quoted in *ABZ* by Mel Gooding

7. *n.* A written representation of the letter. *She grabbed Richard's shoulder, pointed to the device on the wall, the snaky S with the stars surrounding it.* —Neil Gaiman, *Neverwhere*

8. *n.* A device, such as a printer's type, for reproducing the letter.

SCIENTIFIC MATTERS

9. *n.* An energy state of an atom, as in "S State." *The outward atom fills its deep s-state with two electrons and pyramidally bonds to its neighbors with p-orbitals.* —Andrew Zangwill, *Physics at Surfaces*

10. *n.* (thermodynamics) Entropy, or energy unavailable for work.

11. *n.* (chemistry) The symbol for the element sulfur in the periodic table.

STUDENT AFFAIRS

12. *n.* A grade in school rating a student's work as satisfactory.

13. *n.* One graded or rated with an S.

14. *n.* A medieval Roman numeral for 70.

15. *n.* Something arbitrarily designated S (e.g., a person, place, or other thing).

CONTRACTIONS 'S

16. Belongs to. *whale's belly.*

17. Is. *'S not impossible.* —Neil Gaiman, *Neverwhere*

18. Does. *What's he want this time?*

19. Us. *Let's eat.*

20. Has. *He's seen them already.*

21. God, used as a mild oath. *'s blood*

22. As. *so's you can come.*

MISCELLANEOUS

23. *n.* Any spoken sound represented by the letter.
    The sound vibration of the consonant S means "one half of eternity." —Joseph E. Rael, *Tracks of Dancing Light: A Native American Approach to Understanding Your Name*
    She said thee *for* see *not because she had a lisp but because she knew the hissing letter S is the part of a whisper most likely to be overheard.* —C. S. Lewis, *The Last Battle*

24. *n.* The nineteenth letter of the alphabet.
    On the prow of the boat is seated a woman lavishly clad and surrounded by sacks of gold . . . ; in place of

her head is the letter S. —Georges Perec, *Life:*
A User's Manual
"Do you see anything else?" Sylvia shook her head
in bewilderment. "Only the letter S. All I see is an
S. I don't know what it means." —Antoinette May,
Haunted Houses of California: A Ghostly Guide to
Haunted Houses and Wandering Spirits

25. *n.* The nineteenth in a series.

26. *n.* The nineteenth section in a piece of music.

SHAPES AND SIZES

27. *n.* Something having the shape of an S.
    She had this very distinctive shape, seemingly com-
    prised of interlocking S's and C's that made her look
    like she would fit exactly against him if he were to
    embrace her. —Jeremy Dyson, *Never Trust a Rabbit*
    Mara clapped his hands and the flames vanished. In
    their place, its swaying head held at almost twice
    the height of a man, its silver hood fanned, the
    mechobra drew into its S-shaped strike position.
    —Roger Zelazny, *Lord of Light*
    "Hey, can any of you guys do this?" I asked, twisting
    my lips to form the letter "S." —Leslie Cohen, *Jew-*
    ish Love Stories for Kids

28. *n.* S curve: a double curve, as in a road, often dif-
    ficult for drivers to negotiate.
    Carol A. Braddock recalls a time when the road's
    dangerous S-curve ate up at least one vehicle per
    week, with fast-moving drivers ending up wrecked
    in the woods. —Jason B. Grosky, *Eagle-Tribune,*
    April 13, 2004

29. *n.* S bend: see S trap.

30. *n.* S trap: a section of plumbing pipe with an S-shape whose purpose is to trap sewer gases.

31. *n.* S hook: a strip of metal bent into an S-shape.

32. *n.* S twist: "the twist in yarn induced by a counter-clockwise-spinning spindle, sometimes called a crossband twist." —Dr. John Burkardt

33. *n.* S brake: an S-shaped wheel-braking mechanism.

34. *n.* S wrench: a wrench with an S-shaped twist.

35. *n.* S bridge: a double-curved bridge used in early-nineteenth-century road construction to cross curving streams with uneven banks.

FOREIGN MEANINGS

36. *n.* (French) Zigzag, as in *faire des S,* "to go in zigzag fashion."

T IN PRINT AND PROVERB

1. (phrase) *To cross the t's* means to be minutely exact.

2. (in literature) *"We could manage this matter to a T."* (meaning perfectly). —Laurence Sterne, *Tristram Shandy*

3. (in literature) *"T is viceregal lodge."* —James Joyce, *Ulysses*

4. (in literature) *"T is a hammer."* —Victor Hugo, quoted in *ABZ* by Mel Gooding

5. *adv.* Exactly, as in "It suits you to a T."
   He pushed Ottomar Fuldam's portrait to one side and, lo and behold! A tasty smell of cooking wafted out of a hole behind. No sooner did I see the hole than a head popped up—and please don't fall from your chair for a third time—it resembled the head in Ottomar Fuldam's portrait to a "T"! —Wolfgang Bauer, *The Feverhead*

6. *n.* A written representation of the letter.

7. *n.* A device, such as a printer's type, for reproducing the letter.

SQUARES AND OTHER SHAPES

8. *n.* Something having the shape of a T.
   There was a person standing right next to the embankment, describing a large T in the night with two blazing torches! —Wolfgang Bauer, *The Feverhead*
   A map. A broken T scribed with city streets and strings of numbers. It reminds her of a steak's T-bone, the upright tapering raggedly, the left crossarm truncated. Within its outline are avenues,

squares, circles, a long rectangle suggesting a park.
—William Gibson, *Pattern Recognition*
He had a hairy chest, and the hair had a nice, natural pattern to it, across his chest and then a trail down his stomach, a T. —Augusten Burroughs, *Sellevision: A Novel*

9. *n.* T-bone: a thick loin steak containing a T-shaped bone.
Before Lieutenant Breeze (Richard Lane) can arrest Mrs. Murdock for slaying her husband, however, she accidentally chokes to death on a piece of T-bone steak—a rather implausible, if convenient, way of disposing of the villainess. —Gene D. Phillips, *Creatures of Darkness: Raymond Chandler, Detective Fiction, and Film Noir*

10. *n.* T-bone crash: a side-impact car crash, the two cars forming a T-shape.
[S]ide-impact or T-bone crashes—where one car slams into the side of another—kill an estimated 9,000 people a year in the United States. —Jerry Edgerton, *Car Shopping Made Easy*

11. *n.* T bar: 1. a rolled metal beam with a cross section. 2. a piece of body jewelry used in piercing. 3. a type of ski lift. 4. a car roof design which includes two sunroofs. 5. a T-shaped shoe strap.
[A] fast-rising sporting-goods magnate by the name of T Bar Waites. —David James Duncan, *The Brothers K*

12. *n.* T top: a T-shaped car roof design, as in a Corvette.
I dreamed of pulling a real 1979 Corvette T-Top out of that cool, yellow and blue building. —Tim Walsh, *The Playmakers: Amazing Origins of Timeless Toys*

13. *n.* T roof: a T-shaped car roof design, as in a Thunderbird.
Highlights from this incredibly successful three-

*year run included the introduction of a sporty
"T-roof" option in the spring of 1978.* —Mike Mueller,
Thunderbird Milestones

14. *n.* T formation: an offensive football lineup.
*The Bears returned to the finals in 1940, at the
beginning of pro football's modern era with the
formal unveiling of the T-formation.* —Dale Rater-
mann, *Football Crossroads*

15. *n.* T cushion: "the technical name for the remov-
able cushion in a stuffed chair, which looks like a
very broad and squat T" —Dr. John Burkardt

16. *n.* T cart: an open 2-seat, 4-wheeled carriage whose
body is T-shaped.
*He bought an expensive new saddle horse named
Fritz of which he was inordinately proud and
a "very stylish" new T-cart for drives in the park.*
—David McCullough, *Mornings on Horseback: The
Story of an Extraordinary Family, a Vanished Way
of Life and the Unique Child Who Became Theodore
Roosevelt*

17. *n.* T hinge: a hinge in the shape of the letter T.
*A close relative of the strap hinge is the T hinge,
which is like a strap hinge on one side, and a butt
hinge on the other.* —John Holloway, *Illustrated
Theatre Production Guide*

18. *n.* T iron: a rod with a crosspiece at the end used as
a hook.

19. *n.* T dress: a T-shirt long enough to be worn as a dress.

20. *n.* T joint (also tee joint): an electrical connection
between a main conductor and a branch conductor.

21. *n.* T head: a flat-headed bolt.
    Bruder said nothing, the nails stored between his teeth, a T-head bolt behind each ear. —David Ebershoff, *Pasadena: A Novel*

22. *n.* T-head pier: "a pier in the shape of a capital T, with a single walkway extending from the shore, which then terminates in a transverse section" —Dr. John Burkardt
    Nolan followed a service hallway which led to the employees' lounge at the end of the T-head pier. —Matt Braun, *The Overlords*

23. *n.* T bevel: "an adjustable gauge with a wood or plastic handle and a metal blade that pivots out. —eHow.com

24. *n.* T-beam bridge: "a reinforced concrete bridge made of a single slab whose cross-section at the supports resembles a series of T's." —Dr. John Burkardt

25. *n.* T back: a style of bathing suit that forms a T shape in the back.
    So in walks these three guys in nothing but T-back bathing suits. —Patrika Vaughn, *Everything You Need to Know to Write, Publish, and Market Your Book*

26. *n.* T bolt: a bolt with a sharp T-shaped profile.

27. *n.* T nut: a nut that is T-shaped.

28. *n.* T rail: a rail with a T-shaped cross-section.

29. *n.* T plate: "a T-shaped plate used as a splice and for stiffening a joint where the end of one beam abuts against the side of another." —Dr. John Burkardt

30. *n.* T maze: "a simple maze whose blind alleys end in short left and right turns, so that it looks as though it were constructed from a collection of T's, or, to a computer scientist, constructed through recursive application of the T function." —Dr. John Burkardt *In a T-maze a mouse may turn to the right (R) and receive a mild shock, or to the left (L) and get a piece of cheese.* —Abe Mizrahi and Michael Sullivan, *Mathematics: An Applied Approach, 7th Ed.*

31. *n.* T slot: an indentation in wood, for example, that allows accessories to be positioned or follow a track.

32. *n.* T square: a ruler with a crosspiece used to draw horizontal lines and to hold triangles for vertical lines.

33. *n.* T strap: a T-shaped part of an open shoe formed by a strap rising from the throat over the instep and fastening to an ankle strap." —Dr. John Burkardt

34. *n.* T tube: a T-shaped rubber tube, "used to drain the common bile duct." —Dr. John Burkardt

35. *n.* T wrench: a T-shaped wrench whose handle is comprised of a socket that can turn a nut.

36. *n.* Meridian angle.

CONTRACTION 'T

37. It. *'Twas the night before Christmas.*

38. To.
That's why I came t' get you. —Haruki Murakami, *Hard-Boiled Wonderland and the End of the World*

39. The. *one or t'other.*

SCIENTIFIC MATTERS

40. *n.* (biology) Thymine, one of the four nitrogenous bases found in DNA nucleotides.

41. *n.* (biology) T mycoplasma: a virus-like microorganism whose shape suggests a letter T.

42. *n.* A computer hacker attack, also known as "differential cryptanalysis," involving "a complicated series of mathematical assaults that required lots of chosen plaintext (meaning that the attacker needed to have matched sets of original dispatches and encrypted output)." —Steven Levy, *Crypto: How the Code Rebels Beat the Government—Saving Privacy in the Digital Age*

43. *n.* (medicine) T bandage: "a T-shaped bandage used around the waist or perineum." —Dr. John Burkardt

44. *n.* (electronics) T connector: a type of electrical binding post.

45. *n.* (electronics) T joint: "an electrical connection used for joining a branch conductor to a main conductor which continues beyond the branch." —Dr. John Burkardt

46. *n.* (botany) T budding (also shield budding): "a plant budding in which an oval piece of bark bearing a scion bud is fitted into a T-shaped opening in the bark of the stock." —Dr. John Burkardt

MISCELLANEOUS

47. *n.* Something arbitrarily designated T (e.g., a person, place, or other thing).

48. *n.* Someone called T.

T—, one of the great young surfers, turns up one day with a three-wheel trunk motorcycle, the kind drugstore delivery boys use ... and he's got every pill and capsule you ever imagined. —Tom Wolfe, *The Electric Kool-Aid Acid Test*

T simply did not want to leave quickly and quietly. —Al Lutz, "Miceage.com"

49. *n.* The twentieth in a series.

50. *n.* A medieval Roman numeral for 160.

51. *n.* A biblical sign for the number 300.

Three hundred contains the symbol of crucifix-ion. The letter T is the sign for three hundred. —Andrew Louth, *Genesis 1–11: Ancient Christian Commentary on Scripture*

52. *n.* Any spoken sound represented by the letter.

The sound vibration of the consonant T means "time, crystallized light, speeding light that is slowed down light." —Joseph E. Rael, *Tracks of Dancing Light: A Native American Approach to Understanding Your Name*

53. *n.* The twentieth letter of the alphabet.

Without benefit of the stereoscope, by combining the remembered image with the one before her she was able to distinguish the letter T "coming towards me." —Edward Twitchell Hall, *Beyond Culture*

54. *n.* A designation.

We were driving the Lincoln, which didn't have the "T-series" license plates or stickers, or anything to identify it as a Car Service vehicle. —Jonathan Lethem, *Motherless Brooklyn*

55. *n.* The twentieth section in a piece of music.

56. *n.* T-ball (also tee ball): a league sport like baseball designed chiefly for younger players, in which the ball is placed on a tee at home plate instead of being pitched.

57. *n.* (accounting) The simplest form of an account. *In its simplest form, an account consists of three parts: (1) the title of the account, (2) a left or debit side, and (3) a right or credit side. Because the alignment of these parts of an account resembles the letter T, it is referred to as a T account.* —Paul D. Kimmel, *Financial Accounting: Tools for Business Decision Making*

FACTS AND FIGURES

58. Until 1827, thieves were often branded on the thumb with a T.

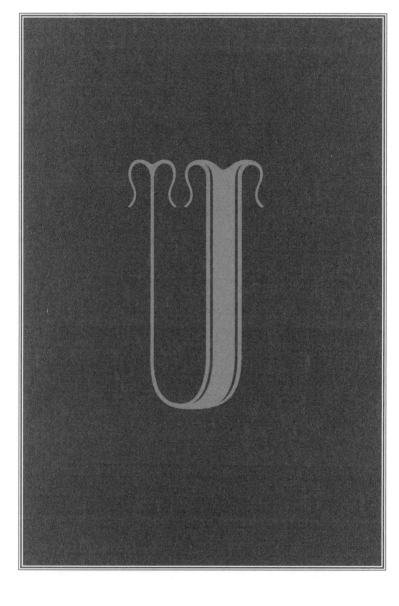

U IN PRINT AND PROVERB

1. **(in literature)** *"The last of the five vowels, If 'you' repeat them; or the fifth, if I."* —William Shakespeare, *Love's Labor's Lost,* V.i.54. There is a pun on *U* and *you.*

2. **(in literature)** *"U, cycles, divine vibrations of dark green oceans,/Peacefulness of pastures dotted with animals, the peace of wrinkles/Which alchemy prints on studious foreheads."* —Arthur Rimbaud, "Vowels"

3. **(in literature)** *"He had looked up through the stinging rain into the dark haze above him, and a giant letter U had filled the sky. He was about to be swallowed up by the mysterious forces of the Devil's Triangle."* —Jimmy Buffett, *Where Is Joe Merchant?: A Novel Tale*

4. **(in literature)** *"U is the urn."* —Victor Hugo, quoted in *ABZ* by Mel Gooding

5. *adj.* **(informal)** Characteristic of the upper class.

6. *n.* A written representation of the letter.

7. *n.* A device, such as a printer's type, for reproducing the letter.

SHAPELY SUBJECTS

8. *n.* Something having the shape of a U, as in a crescent moon.
It was south of New York by nine degrees of latitude, which should have been enough to make a difference in the angle of the moon in the sky, I figured. The crescent would be turned clockwise slightly tonight, so that it would look more like the letter U

than the letter C it had been the night before in New York. —John Berendt, *Midnight in the Garden of Good and Evil*

The hotel was basically a thick letter U, with the base of the U on Broadway and the arms of the U on the side streets. . . . The U started with floor seventeen and went on up that way, so all the hotel rooms could have windows. —Donald E. Westlake, *What's the Worst That Could Happen?*

9. *n.* U turn: a turn made by a vehicle into the opposite direction.
   Another well-meant but unpleasant habit of Herschel's is the way he takes up your ideas, identifies with them, expands upon them, develops their implications, drives them on like an old Ford so that soon they seem to have taken a U-turn into another identity: not even the year or the make are the same. —William H. Gass, The Tunnel

10. *n.* A valley resulting from glacial erosion.
    The shoreline receded, forming a giant U valley. —Piers Anthony, Up in a Heaval: A Xanth Novell

11. *n.* U boat: a military submarine.
    Although Admiral Karl Doenitz, commander of the German U-boat fleet, was surprised by Pearl Harbor and the entry of the United States into the war, he quickly improvised a plan for attack across the Atlantic. Sensing a great opportunity, he proposed sending twelve U-boats to American waters. —Homer Hickam, Torpedo Junction: U-Boat War Off America's East Coast, 1942

12. *n.* U bolt: a bolt with two threaded arms (for attaching nuts).

13. *n.* U lock: a U-shaped bicycle lock.
    Although heavy and ugly, the frame-mounted U-lock is one of the best ways of stopping thieves from going off with your bike. —Fred Milson, *Complete Bike Maintenance*

14. *n.* U rail: a U-shaped rail.

15. *n.* U-shaped bottom: a pattern of stock market activity that drops quickly, hovers at a low point, and then sharply recovers.

16. *n.* U stirrup: a U-shaped stirrup for reinforced concrete.

17. *n.* U trap: a plumbing device used to trap sewer gas.
    "I expect that this shaft is designed like a U-trap. I bet that the passage rises again—" she pointed at the mysterious doorway in the far wall, *"in fact I can see the first steps even from here."* —Wilbur Smith, *The Seventh Scroll*

18. *n.* U tube: a tube that branches into two sections.

19. (music) A harp that has a U-shaped wooden frame, through which the musician strings strands of his or her own hair.

HEY, U

20. *n.* Something arbitrarily designated U (e.g., a person, place, or other thing).

21. *pronoun.* (informal) You, as in "I O U" and "Tune Up While U Wait."

MISCELLANEOUS

22. *n.* Any spoken sound represented by the letter.
    The sound vibration of the vowel U means "to carry,
    carrying light." —Joseph E. Rael, Tracks of Dancing
    Light: A Native American Approach to Understand-
    ing Your Name

23. *n.* The twenty-first letter of the alphabet.
    Murray worked ceaselessly on his [Oxford English]
    dictionary for thirty-six years. . . . He was work-
    ing on the letter u when he died. —Bill Bryson, The
    Mother Tongue

24. *n.* The twenty-first in a series.

25. *n.* The twenty-first section in a piece of music.

26. *n.* Dream consciousness.
    And so we come to the letter U [of the sacred Hindu
    syllable AUM], which is said to represent the field
    and state of Dream Consciousness, where, although
    subject and object may appear to be different and
    separate from each other, they are actually one
    and the same. —Joseph Campbell, The Mythic
    Image

SCIENTIFIC MATTERS

27. *n.* (thermodynamics) Intrinsic energy.

28. *n.* (chemistry) The symbol for the element ura-
    nium in the periodic table.

29. *n.* (biology) Uracil, one of the four nitrogenous
    bases found in RNA nucleotides.

30. *n.* (mathematics) A matrix with special properties. *U is an echelon matrix.* —Marie A. Vitulli, "A Brief History of Linear Algebra and Matrix Theory"

FOREIGN MEANINGS

31. *n.* (French) Stirrup-shaped, as in *en U.*

32. *n.* (Burmese) A title of respect, used before a man's proper name.

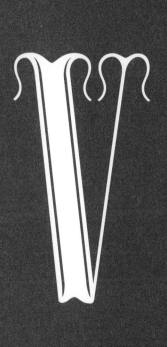

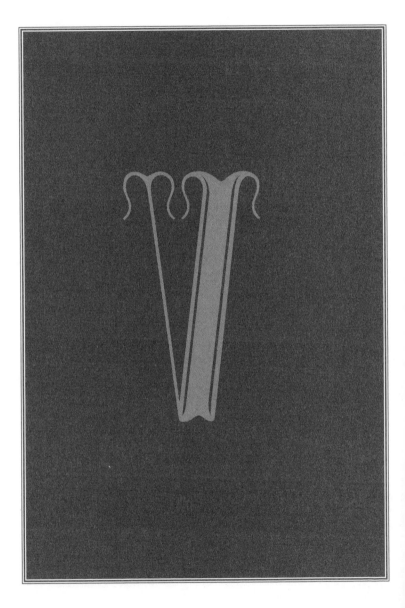

V IN PRINT AND PROVERB

1. (in literature) *V and Other Poems* (1991) collects the work of Tony Harrison.

2. (in literature) *"V is the vase."* —Victor Hugo, quoted in *ABZ* by Mel Gooding

3. **(in music)** Haydn's Symphony 88 is known as "The Letter V Symphony."

4. *n.* A written representation of the letter.

5. *n.* A device, such as a printer's type, for reproducing the letter.

IT ALL ADDS UP

6. *n.* **(informal)** A five-dollar bill.

7. *n.* The twenty-second in a series.

8. *n.* A Roman numeral for five.
   I have lost a Roman numeral somewhere. V for the vee between. —William H. Gass, The Tunnel
   The Roman numeral representing five, symbolized by the letter V, derives from the shape of the space between the open thumb and fingers. The Roman numeral for ten, the letter X, is actually two V's.
   —Michael S. Schneider, A Beginner's Guide to Constructing the Universe: Mathematical Archetypes of Nature, Art, and Science

9. *n.* With a line over it, **a Roman numeral for 5,000.**

10. *n.* In mathematics, the sign of the triangle (representing an angle); the sign of the compass.

MISCELLANEOUS

11. *n.* Any spoken sound represented by the letter.
    *The sound vibration of the consonant V means
    "descending light."* —Joseph E. Rael, *Tracks of Danc-
    ing Light: A Native American Approach to Under-
    standing Your Name*

12. *n.* The twenty-second letter of the alphabet.
    *I've been traveling along the Zuider Zee in search of
    the V in the V.* —William H. Gass, *The Tunnel*

13. *n.* An arm signal indicating that help is needed.
    *Arms up in the shape of a letter 'V' means "I/We
    need help."* —John Mock, *Lonely Planet: Hiking in
    the Sierra Nevada*

14. *n.* Potential difference.

15. *n.* Something arbitrarily designated V (e.g., a per-
    son, place, or other thing).

16. *n.* A talisman for high academic success.
    *A young lad came to college as a freshman and
    checked into his room. The first thing he did was
    hammer a big brass letter V on his door. Everybody
    asked him what it was for, but he wouldn't tell them.
    He kept it polished, and it was always the first thing
    put up in his room as he moved from dorm to dorm.
    Finally he graduated and at the commencement
    exercise, his name was announced as valedictorian.
    When he walked across the stage, there in his left
    hand was his polished brass letter V.* —Robert Schul-
    ler, *Tough Times Never Last, but Tough People Do!*

17. *n.* (chemistry) The symbol for the element vana-
    dium in the periodic table.

18. *n.* The twenty-second section in a piece of music.

19. *n.* A ripple of water.
Ducks pulled rippling Vs across the brackish water.
—Jeremy Dyson, *Never Trust a Rabbit*

20. *n.* An angled window.
Those panes of glass angle in toward each other to form a self-regarding V. —Jerry Herron, "Niki's Window"

MILITARY

21. *n.* A robot bomb, as the World War II German V-1.
The V-1 "robot bomb," or, as the British called it, "buzz bomb," was the predecessor of the modern cruise missile. —Stephen Tanner, *Refuge from the Reich: American Airmen and Switzerland During World War II*

22. *n.* A warship designation in the fleet's inventory.
The letter V indicated that the squadron flew heavier-than-air vehicles. This designation was a relic of naval aviation's early days when helium-filled dirigibles appeared to be permanent fixtures in the fleet. —James D. Hornfischer, *The Last Stand of the Tin Can Sailors: The Extraordinary World War II Story of the U.S. Navy's Finest Hour*

23. *n.* V sign: a victory salute made by forming the index and middle fingers into a V shape.
There was some undeniable truth in Clare Booth Luce's remark, "All famous men have their characteristic gestures. Churchill had his V sign. Hitler his upraised arm, and Roosevelt..." Whereupon she moistened her index finger and held it aloft to test the wind. —Gordon W. Prange, *Pearl Harbor: The Verdict of History*

POINTED DISCUSSIONS

24. *n.* Something having the shape of a V.
   *Rosemary said the object appeared to be similar
   to two lampshades inside a wide V, with the light
   from the lampshades brighter than that from the
   V.* —Don Ledger, "UFO Comes into Close Proximity
   with Vehicle Near Day's Corner"
   *He lounged in his leather chair, content, with his
   legs straight out in front of him in a tremendous letter V.* —Martha Stout, *The Myth of Sanity: Divided
   Consciousness and the Promise of Awareness*
   *The woman's face was so narrow that her smile was
   almost V-shaped.* —Pat Cadigan, *Dervish Is Digital*

25. *n.* V block: a steel block with a V-shaped groove,
   used in machine tooling.

26. *n.* V bottom: a broad sailboat or speedboat.
   *When we speak of V-bottom boats, most people think
   of a high-speed motorboat.* —Ted Brewer, *Understanding Boat Design*

27. *n.* V cut: a style of dress.
   *Her dresses were cut in a deep V like the style you
   see in Lautrec's posters of Yvette Guilbert.* —William H. Gass, *The Tunnel*

28. *n.* V hut: a primitive shelter in the shape of an
   inverted V.
   *Other impressive constructions on the site include
   a number of underground chambers with clear
   astronomical alignments, including . . . a classic V-hut chamber, above ground, wedge shaped
   and adjacent to a large basin cut into the bedrock.*
   —Paul Tudor Angel, "Mystery Hill: America's
   Stonehenge"

29. *n.* V-neck: the V-shaped neck of a sweater.
*The world's oldest preserved textile garment is a
5,000-year-old linen shirt from an Egyptian tomb at
Tarkhan. The man's shirt was intentionally V-necked,
perhaps to expose the throat and clavicle bones.*
—David B. Givens, Center for Nonverbal Studies

30. *n.* V-neck: a patented style of guitar neck.
*The heart of the new v-neck is the double "T" rail
extrusion that begins at the V-shaped headstock
and runs the entire length of the fingerboard to the
22nd fret.* —Vaccaro Guitars

31. *n.* V aerial: an antenna shaped like a V.
*[The pink stretch limo had] gold-tint mirror glass,
and a flying-V aerial on the back. Very cyberpunk.*
—Ian McDonald, *Evolution's Shore*

32. *n.* V-beam radar: "a height-finding radar that
emits a vertical beam and another at 45 degrees."
—Dr. John Burkardt

33. *n.* V belt: "a belt with a V-shaped cross section
which engages a similarly shaped groove in a pul-
ley." —Dr. John Burkardt

34. *n.* V bob: "a strong frame shaped like an isosceles
triangle, turning on a pivot at its apex, and used
as a bell crank to change the direction of a main
pump rod." —Dr. John Burkardt

35. *n.* V roof: a gable or peaked roof.
*They are then marched around one building
toward another that has a single door directly
under the inverted V of the roof.* —Ian MacMillan,
*Village of a Million Spirits: A Novel of the Treblinka
Uprising*

36. *n.* V guideway: "a slotted path, with V-shaped indentations in the sides. A weight-bearing pallet is placed in the path. It has corresponding V-shaped projections which keep it firmly held within the path. It then glides along the path, carrying some load." —Dr. John Burkardt

37. *n.* V hook: the V-shaped opening of an eccentric rod in a steam engine.

38. *n.* V moth: a moth whose wings feature a V-shaped mark.

39. *n.* V notch: in a triangular weir, a notch used to measure water flow.
    A V-notch weir across a stream or ditch consists of a weir, which retains the water, with a notch, through which the water flows. —William J. Sutherland, *The Conservation Handbook*

40. *n.* V particle: a subatomic particle named for the shape of its track in a cloud chamber.

41. *n.* V-type engine: a type of internal combustion engine in which the cylinders are arranged in a V shape (e.g., V-6 or V-8).
    Cadillac anticipated the advantages of the V-type engine back in 1914 and has built no other type since. —R. M. Clarke, *Cadillac Automobiles 1949–1959*

42. *n.* V pug: a moth whose wings feature a V-shaped mark.

43. *n.* V-shaped bottom: a stock market pattern involving a sharp drop followed by an almost immediate and similarly sharp recovery.

44. *n.* V-shaped comb: a comb on some domestic fowl with two hornlike sections that form a V.

45. *n.* V stern: "a square stern with the transom inclined from the vertical." —Dr. John Burkardt

46. *n.* V tail: a V-shaped airplane tail.
[S]ome pilots claimed the V-tail caused excessive fishtailing in turbulence. —Larry Lehmer, *The Day the Music Died: The Last Tour of Buddy Holly, the Big Bopper, and Ritchie Valens*

47. *n.* V thread: a screw thread of 60 degrees.

48. *n.* V tool: a woodworking tool for carving grooves.

49. *n.* V vat: a funnel box.

50. *n.* A mountain cleft.
At last a cleft opened, a narrow V between a near hill and the distant peak behind it. —Stan McDaniel, *The Letterseeker*

FACTS AND FIGURES

51. "The V in cricket is the area of the field that falls between mid on and mid off." —Dr. John Burkardt

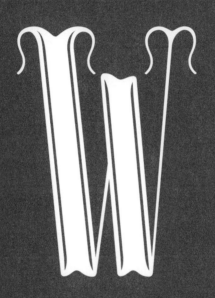

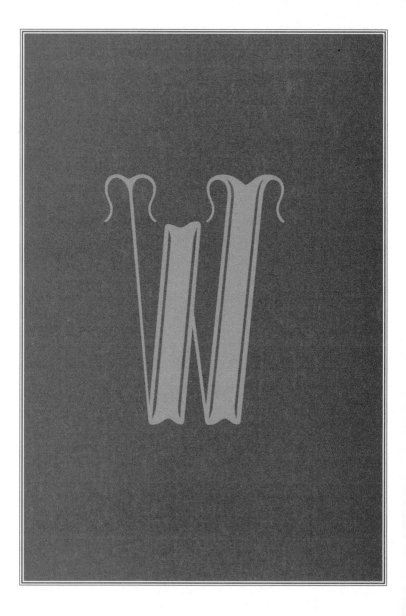

W IN PRINT AND PROVERB

1. **(in literature)** *" 'Are you the only man in the world that never must go to the W?' she would jeer."* —D. H. Lawrence, *Mr. Noon.* The *W* here is short for "water closet."

2. **(in literature)** *"Reasonable old Bertram, always trying to throw oil on the troubled w's."* —P. G. Wodehouse, *Right Ho, Jeeves.* The *w* here is short for *waters.*

3. **(in literature)** *"And sprawling W's, and V's, and Y's, / Gaped prodigiously."* —Robert Southey, quoted in *The Alphabet Abecedarium* by Richard Firmage

4. *n.* A written representation of the letter.

5. *n.* A device, such as a printer's type, for reproducing the letter.

SCIENTIFIC MATTERS

6. *n.* **(biology)** Tryptophan, an amino acid.

7. *n.* **(biology)** A female sex chromosome in which the female has two kinds of sex chromosomes.

8. *n.* **(chemistry)** The symbol for the element tungsten in the periodic table.

PEOPLE, PLACES, THINGS

9. *n.* something arbitrarily designated W (e.g., a person, place, or other thing).
   Books you were going to write with letters for titles. Have you read his F? O yes, but I prefer Q. Yes, but W is wonderful. O yes, W. —James Joyce, *Ulysses*

> *Should I marry W.? Not if she won't tell me the other letters in her name.* —Woody Allen, *The Complete Prose of Woody Allen*

10. *n.* The twenty-third in a series.

11. *n.* Something having the shape of a W.
> *But the ironical thing, which could have been fore-seen long ago, is that the [puzzle] piece the dead man holds between his fingers is shaped like a W.* —Georges Perec, *Life: A User's Manual*
> *He remembered seeing from the air that there were two or three small lakes among them, one almost as large as the one on which he had landed earlier, but shaped like a crooked, flattened letter W.* —Sue Henry, *Sleeping Lady: An Alex Jensen Mystery*

12. *n.* Someone called W.
> *Still, they seemed to get along politely enough, Miss H serving Mrs. W tea in the drawing room with a civility that was one notch up from frosty, and Mrs. W seeming slightly embarrassed and modestly grateful.* —Iain Banks, *The Business*

MISCELLANEOUS

13. *n.* Any spoken sound represented by the letter.
> *The sound vibration of the consonant W means "two ways of descending light."* —Joseph E. Rael, *Tracks of Dancing Light: A Native American Approach to Understanding Your Name*
> *Like his father, and Grandfather Darwin as well, he tended to stammer, having special difficulties with the letter w.* —E. Janet Browne, *Charles Darwin: Voyaging*

14. *n.* The twenty-third letter of the English alphabet.
File me under W / because I wonce / was / a woman.
—Marge Piercy, "The Secretary Chant"

15. *n.* "Double U" or "double V."

16. *n.* Terror; the mark of death.
Terror is a one letter word—W. —Tagline for the
1974 film *W,* directed by Richard Quine

17. *n.* The twenty-third section in a piece of music.

18. *n.* W engine: "an internal combustion engine with
three sets of cylinders arranged side by side in
three planes so that a cross section would have the
shape of a W." —Dr. John Burkardt

X IN PRINT AND PROVERB

1. **(in literature)** In *Rootabaga Stories*, Carl Sandburg tells how the letter X was invented by "the men who change the alphabets." In three separate stories, these men create the X to represent crossed fingers, wildcat claws, and crossed arms.

2. **(in literature)** In Joseph Conrad's *Secret Agent*, Professor X is an anarchist who fastens explosives to himself so that he can kill himself and anyone nearby at the touch of a button.

3. **(in literature)** *The Man Who Broke Out of the Letter X* is a 1984 novel by Robert Priest.

4. **(in literature)** As a sociable letter: *"The letter X is equally sociable [to O], because it too neighbors most of the letter, and avoids only 8 of them."* —Simon Singh, *The Code Book: The Science of Secrecy from Ancient Egypt to Quantum Cryptography*

5. **(in literature)** As a harsh letter: *"He is, as I see it and in my opinion, Amiable, Benevolent, Courteous, Dignified, Enamored, Firm, Gallant, Honorable, Illustrious, Loyal, Manly, Noble, Openhearted, Pleasing, Quick-witted, Rich, the Ss that everybody knows, and then Truthful, Valiant, X isn't included because it's a harsh letter, Y is the same I, and Z is Zealous in protecting your honor."* —Miguel de Cervantes, *Don Quixote*

6. **(in literature)** *"X is Davy's publichouse in upper Leeson street."* —James Joyce, *Ulysses*

7. **(in literature)** the main character in *Composition No. 1: A Novel,* by Marc Saporta. " *'The apartment door opens on a long slender figure in a black hat.' X visiting Marianne, who says 'My nose is my despair.*

I wish it were shorter.' X thinks: 'How to keep from telling her . . . that she is wonderfully desirable?' " (from the reading notes by Nick Montfort).

8. **(in literature)** As a fatal letter: *"Most cultural and linguistic investments in the letter x carry the grain of something inherently fatal."* —Marina Roy, *Sign After the X*

9. **(in literature)** *"X is crossed swords, a battle: who will win we do not know, so the mystics made it the sign of destiny and the algebraists the sign of the unknown."* —Victor Hugo, quoted in *ABZ* by Mel Gooding

10. *n.* Distance between top and bottom of a printed letter without an ascender or descender.

11. *n.* A final judgment day taught by the Church of the SubGenius in the book *Revelation X,* in which alien saucers arrive on earth to initiate the end times (also known as "the Rupture"). *What happens when X-Day comes and goes, and the saucers haven't shown?* —Mitchell Porter

12. *n.* A written representation of the letter.

13. *n.* A device, such as a printer's type, for reproducing the letter.

CARDS, LIQUOR, ADULT MOVIES

14. *n.* A playing card of low rank.

15. *adj.* (obsolete) A motion picture rating prohibiting admittance of anyone under 17 years old. (See *G, R.*) *[T]he R-rated brotherly chat for which he'd detoured through Seattle was in danger of being*

*preempted by Everett's conflicting role in an even-
tually to be X-rated performance with the Sad Abdomen Lady!* —David James Duncan, *The Brothers K*

16. *adj.* Strength of ale (X being weakest, XXX being
strongest).
*Florence MacCabe takes a crubeen and a bottle of
double X for supper every Saturday.* —James Joyce,
Ulysses

ON PARCHMENT PAPER

17. *n.* A kiss, put at the end of a personal letter.
You can count the Xs as kisses. —Julian Barnes,
Staring at the Sun

18. *n.* A signature, such as an illiterate person's.
*The town I was born in was made by a crossing of
tracks. A rare and momentous event, this intersection, for those two tracks had passed over mile
after mile of prairie as if the earth they lay on were
space through which they were falling—two lives,
two histories, two kinds of loneliness—with no idea
they were converging, and must cross; yet in the
moment of their meeting they were silent, for what
did they compose then but an illiterate's X?* —William H. Gass, *The Tunnel*

19. *n.* A precise point on a map or diagram, as in "X
marks the spot."
*X marks the place where victims fall / as well as
buried treasure.* —Rebecca McClanahan, "X"

20. *n.* Incorrect answer (as on a test); mistake.

21. *v.* To cross out.
I passed through the month the way people X out

days on a calendar, one after the one. —Haruki
Murakami, *A Wild Sheep Chase*

22. *v.* To mark with an X.
    Jane is the fourth from the left (an X over her head
    shows which she is, otherwise hard to recognise her).
    —Georges Perec, *Life: A User's Manual*

23. *v.* To indicate a choice (as on a ballot).

24. *n.* An indication of where to sign one's name.
    "Sign there," he says, his dirty finger on the red X.
    —Edward Abbey, *The Fool's Progress*

CHRIS CROSS

25. *n.* Crossed swords.
    X signifies crossed swords, combat—who will be vic-
    tor? Nobody knows—that is why philosophers used x
    to signify fate, and the mathematicians took it for the
    unknown. —Victor Hugo, *Voyages and Excursions*

26. *n.* Christ, as in Xmas, or Xian.

27. *n.* The word *Chris.*

28. *n.* Something arbitrarily designated X.
    Everyone wants a consoling myth. And the consolation
    either takes the form of an assurance that X, whatever
    it was when, like every dog, it had its day, was singu-
    lar, solitary, and unique, and that nothing like it could
    possibly happen again; or it imitates the pooh-pooh of
    condescension . . . , insisting that things like X happen
    all the time, almost nonstop if you are so stupid as to
    have to be told. —William H. Gass, *The Tunnel*
    That x only looks like an x, something I know well.
    In fact it is a manifestation of y, something I don't.

—Nick Curry, explaining "the deep otherness of the superficially familiar things" a Westerner sees in Japan—"Superlegitimacy: Passion and Ecstasy of a Tokyo Train Driver," IMomus.com

29. *n.* An arbitrary point in time.
How many millions have been murdered since X?
—William H. Gass, *The Tunnel*

30. *n.* Crossed with.

31. *n.* Something with an X shape, such as a cross.
X-shaped canvas folding chairs with whorled feet.
—Georges Perec, *Life: A User's Manual*
His body had the shape of a sloppy letter X—arms stretched over his head, along the edge of the back pillows, legs open in a wide fork. —Ayn Rand, *The Fountainhead*
My fingers are mated into a mirrored series of what manifests, to me, as the letter X. —David Foster Wallace, *Infinite Jest: A Novel*

32. *n.* A cross-stitch of thread.
My grandmother collected x's in her lap, / canceling the empty muslin with thread and needle, / one stitch by one stitch, until a flower bloomed.
—Rebecca McClanahan, "X"

33. *adj.* Annoyed, angry, irritated, cross (a pun on x's cross shape).

34. *v.* In the game of chess, captures.

35. *v.* To obliterate.

36. *n.* A sign representing "the merging of the physical and spiritual," according to Herman R. Bangerter, "Significance of Ancient, Geometric Symbols."

37. *n.* A hobo sign.
    *The plain "X" meant handout available at nearest
    house.* —Edward Abbey, *The Fool's Progress*

38. *n.* X legs: legs bending inward at the middle.
    *Mary and Joseph were poorly painted blobs, the
    manger was a veed cradle on spindly X legs, the
    shed's slanted roof was grooved to look like wood.*
    —Susan S. Kelly, *Even Now*

39. *n.* X stretcher: an X-shaped support usually used to
    hold four parallel beams at a fixed distance, as the
    legs of a coffee table.

DR./MR./MRS./MS. X

40. *n.* A person or thing of unknown identity.
    *Psychologists and police profilers often tell us that
    fame is a driving rationale for people to commit
    heinous crimes. Murderers and rapists can publish
    firsthand-account books from prison. I would rec-
    ommend that all people convicted of serious crimes
    simply be referred to as Mr. or Mrs. X by the media.
    Real names would be secured within court docu-
    ments and available for legal means. But to the rest
    of the world, the fame would dissipate. What pun-
    ishment or deterrent could be better than erasure
    of one's name?* —Aslan, "No Notoriety for the Noto-
    rious," *Halfbakery.com*

41. *n.* An insignificant person.
    *Only in historical retrospect do we see that some-
    times suddenly a certain insignificant Mr. X, with-
    out knowing it himself, had the whole situation in
    his hands.* —Marie-Louise von Franz, *Archetypal
    Dimensions of the Psyche*

I am Mr. X or Ms. X, I live in X street, like thousands of others, and it really wouldn't make much differ-ence if a few people like me got killed—there's more than enough of us anyway! —Marie-Louise von Franz, *Archetypal Dimensions of the Psyche*

42. *n.* The thirteenth generation to be born since the American Constitution.
Then there's "Generation X," the tag that was affixed to my age bracket by Douglas Coupland in his 1991 novel Generation X: Takes for an Acceler-ated Culture. *Thanks, but no thanks, Doug. Sounds too much like "Brand X." There is a blankness, a lack of identity, even a sense of negation in that big letter X that is disturbing to our self-image.* —Kevin Graham Ford, *Jesus for a New Generation: Putting the Gospel in the Language of Xers*

43. *n.* The archetype of a mad scientist.
Dr. X will build a creature. —The Rocky Horror Picture Show

44. *n.* A person named X.
At one time, they must have all been little pink babies, cute and gurgly, but that was as hard for me to imagine as X being a hippie. —Deborah Ellis, *Looking for X*

SCIENTIFIC MATTERS

45. *n.* A viral encephalitis of man first detected in Aus-tralia. **Also called x-disease.**

46. *n.* **(biology)** Hybrid, or offspring of mixed origin.

47. *n.* In horse breeding, foaled by.

48. *n.* Symbol meaning "experimental."

49. *n.* Chemical group.

50. *n.* A female sex chromosome.
    The X chromosome is one of the two types of human sex chromosomes. The other is called the Y chromosome. If two X chromosomes are present, the person is a female. If an X and a Y chromosome are present, the person is a male. —World Book

51. *n.* Power of magnification: 10*x* means *magnified ten times.*

52. *n.* A unit of radioactive wavelength.

53. *n.* A latent virus.

54. *n.* A halogen molecule group.
    Alkyl groups are often represented by the letter R, just as halogens are often represented by the letter X. —Frank Pellegrini, Organic Chemistry I

55. *n.* (electronics) Reactance.
    Reactance in general is symbolized by the capital letter X. —Stan Gibilisco, Teach Yourself Electricity and Electronics

MATHEMATICS

56. *n.* The Roman numeral 10.

57. *n.* The twenty-fourth in a series.

58. *n.* Abscissa, an x coordinate.
    Conventionally, the abscissa axis is labeled with the letter x and the ordinate axis with the letter y. —Julio Sanchez, DirectX 3D Graphics Programming Bible

59. *n.* In the Cartesian coordinate system, the width axis of a three-dimensional space.

It is common to label the axis representing the width of a three-dimensional space with the letter X, the height axis with the letter Y, and the depth axis with the letter Z. —Isaac Victor Kerlow, *The Art of 3-D Computer Animation and Effects, Third Edition*

60. *n.* The multiplication operator, read "times," as in 7 × 6 = 42.

X was used by William Oughtred (1574–1660) in the Clavis Mathematicae *(Key to Mathematics), composed about 1628 and published in London in 1631.* —Jeff Miller, "Earliest Uses of Various Mathematical Symbols"

61. *prep.* By. 2' × 2' reads *two feet by two.*

62. *n.* Vector product.

X for vector product was used in 1902 in J. W. Gibbs's Vector Analysis *by E. B. Wilson.* —Jeff Miller, "Earliest Uses of Various Mathematical Symbols"

63. *n.* An unknown quantity.

The predominant use of the letter x to represent an unknown value came about in an interesting way. During the printing of La Géométrie *[1637] and its appendix,* Discours de la Méthode, *which introduced coordinate geometry, the printer reached a dilemma. While the text was being typeset, the printer began to run short of the last letters of the alphabet. He asked Descartes if it mattered whether x, y, or z was used in each of the book's many equations. Descartes replied that it made no difference which of the three letters was used to designate an unknown quantity. The printer selected x for most*

*of the unknowns, since the letters y and z are used
in the French language more frequently than is x.*
—Art Johnson, quoted in Jeff Miller, "Earliest Uses
of Various Mathematical Symbols"

FOREIGN MEANINGS

64. *n.* (French) Math. "To be strong in X" or "to have a
head for X" means "to be good in math."

65. *n.* (French) The Polytechnic School in Paris: *l'X.*

66. *n.* (French) "Knock-kneed," as in *Jambes en X.*

MISCELLANEOUS

67. *n.* The unknown; the unknowable.
*But when one realizes that x also stands in for all that
lies beyond the threshold of what is knowable, a pattern begins to emerge.* —Marina Roy, *Sign After the X*

68. *n.* The soul or substance of the universe.
*[The creator] expressed him upon the Universe in
the figure of the letter X.* —Plato, *Timaeus*

69. *n.* Any spoken sound represented by *X.*
*The sound vibration of the consonant X means
"power, empowered."* —Joseph E. Rael, *Tracks of
Dancing Light: A Native American Approach to
Understanding Your Name*

70. *n.* The twenty-fourth letter of the alphabet.
*The Romans . . . may be presumed to have borrowed
West Greek's X partly because it was there.* —Alex-
ander Humez, *A B C Et Cetera*

71. *n.* A warning sign or threat, as concerning live-stock grazing rights.

Expecting to find teeth and claw marks [on the dead calf], instead he found a bullet hole in the calf's back, the letter X carved on its side. —Luanne Rice, *Dream Country*

72. *n.* A shadow of things to come.

May not this letter be a type or sign prepared and designed by God to prefigure some future thing or event, or to be, as St. Paul says, "a shadow of things to come?" —The Ancient Ones of the Earth: Being the History of the Primitive Alphabet

73. *n.* A target.

There was a big letter X marking the spot [for a parachute jump]. It was made from two lengths of shiny red material, weighted down with stones.... [A young man] nodded and beamed smiles at the crowd, who watched in silence as he made his way towards the X, planting the chair down firmly in its center.
—Ian Rankin, *Resurrection Men: An Inspector Rebus Novel*

74. *n.* The twenty-fourth section in a piece of music.

FACTS AND FIGURES

75. Besides being the most versatile one-letter word, *X* is the most printed. From ballots to personal letters to maps to school exams, it seems that *X* can't mark enough spots. And since *X* represents more verbs than any other one-letter word, its active life is appropriate.

76. A king's X is "a 'safe' sign used in children's games. Forming an X with your fingers means that you can't be caught. The phrase is supposed to have come from 'King's excuse.' " —Dr. John Burkardt

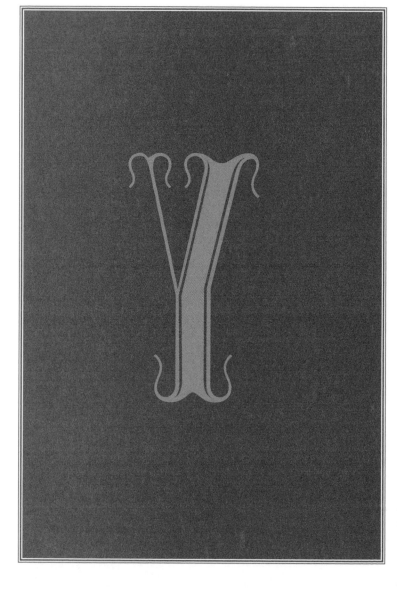

Y IN PRINT AND PROVERB

1. **(in literature)** In Bertolt Brecht's *Private Life of the Master Race*, Y is a German physicist (patterned after Einstein) who fears discovery by the Nazis.

2. **(in literature)** The title of a 2000 film written and directed by Zoe Margolis. The film's description states: "A cross between *Don't Look Now* and *Pulp Fiction*, with a twist of film noir, *Y* unfolds through two parallel narratives and follows a man fated to have premonitions of his own death without realizing it, until it is too late."

3. **(in literature)** As the equivalent to the word I: *"He is, as I see it and in my opinion, Amiable, Benevolent, Courteous, Dignified, Enamored, Firm, Gallant, Honorable, Illustrious, Loyal, Manly, Noble, Openhearted, Pleasing, Quick-witted, Rich, the Ss that everybody knows, and then Truthful, Valiant, X isn't included because it's a harsh letter, Y is the same as I, and Z is Zealous in protecting your honor."*
—Miguel de Cervantes, *Don Quixote*

4. **(in literature)** *"Y is a tree, a fork, the confluence of two rivers, a stemmed glass, a man with arms upstretched."*
—Victor Hugo, quoted in *ABZ* by Mel Gooding

5. **(in print)** The word *why*. Referring to a brand of potato chips named "X" (after Malcolm X), *Entertainment Weekly* magazine asked, "Y?"

6. *n.* A written representation of the letter.
My own [handwritten] y wouldn't have the guts to tie itself to the P like that. —Peter Esterhazy, *Celestial Harmonies: A Novel*
Twenty-seven years had passed between the two inscriptions, but Grandmother's penmanship had not faltered, it was just as sweeping and light

handed. The only difference was in the two y's. The top one, the younger, you might say, was more sophisticated . . . the leg of the y plunges under in a curve, leaning slightly to the right . . . then after a quick loop it pucks up speed, it sweeps back almost to the base of the h, then turns back around. —Peter Esterhazy, *Celestial Harmonies: A Novel*

7. *n.* A device, such as a printer's type, for reproducing the letter.

8. **(in film)** Mind-altering radiation in the 2001 film *The Caveman's Valentine.*
   [T]he solution makes perfect sense to a man who is wracked by "brain typhoons" caused by yellow "Y-beams" and green "Z-beams" emanating from the spires of the Chrysler Building. Somewhere inside that landmark, a mysterious evil mastermind named Cornelius Gould Stuyvesant tracks and torments our hapless hero. —CrankyCritic.com

BY LAND, SEA, AND AIR

9. *n.* A principal railroad track and two diverging branches arranged like the letter Y. With a cross track connecting the diverging branches, it is used in reversing engines or trains.

10. *n.* Something Y-shaped.
    The cyntetokerus is a smallish horse cum deer with a horn on either temple and a long Y-shaped prong at the end of its nose. —Haruki Murakami, *Hardboiled Wonderland and the End of the World*
    [E]ach new moment of life would resemble the letter Y, with the upper branches of the letter representing the two routes or paths available to the individual at the new moment. This moment itself would occur

at the point at which the three branches of the letter meet. —Milton R. Cudney, *Self-Defeating Behaviors: Free Yourself from the Habits, Compulsions, Feelings, and Attitudes That Hold You Back*

11. *n.* A type of highway intersection.
The road ended to the north in a Y. —George Chesbro, *The Language of Cannibals*

12. *n.* An antisubmarine gun having two barrels that form a fork to permit the simultaneous firing of depth charges on each side of the ship.
The Icarus *had been searching, making question marks on the sea, but now she was lined up for her second attack. Jester gave the command and a "V" pattern, one charge from the rack and two from the Y-gun, splashed into the water.* —Homer Hickam, *Torpedo Junction: U-Boat War Off America's East Coast, 1942*

13. *n.* A forked support for a telescope.

PEOPLE, PLACES, THINGS

14. *contraction* (informal) You.
Y' can't argue about that. —Haruki Murakami, *Hardboiled Wonderland and the End of the World*

15. *n.* Something arbitrarily designated Y (e.g., a person, place, or other thing).

16. *n.* The twenty-fifth in a series.

17. *n.* The second in order or class when X is made the first.

18. *n.* An unknown thing; a person of unknown identity.
She is nervous. . . . Suspects X, fears Y. —William H. Gass, *The Tunnel*

19. *n.* A kind of silver moth.

20. *n.* A kind of gapeworm.

21. *n.* Shortened form of Y.M.C.A.
    "Aren't you going to the Y?" —Flannery O'Connor,
    "Everything That Rises Must Converge"

22. *n.* In the Cartesian coordinate system, the height
    axis of a three-dimensional space.
    It is common to label the axis representing the
    width of a three-dimensional space with the letter X,
    the height axis with the letter Y, and the depth axis
    with the letter Z. —Isaac Victor Kerlow, *The Art of*
    3-D Computer Animation and Effects, Third Edition

23. *n.* Medieval Roman numeral for 150.

24. *n.* With a line above it, a Roman numeral for 150,000.

25. *n.* A symbol of communism.
    [I]t is the symbols of Communism that return to
    attack and kill Benny, and in the last lines of [Vene-
    dikt Erofeev's] novel [Moscow Circles], it is the red
    letter "Y" that spreads before Benny's eyes as he
    dies. Throughout the novel, it is this letter that has
    symbolized Benny's participation in the symbolic
    order, as it is the only letter his baby son knows.
    —Avril Tonkin, "Moscow Circles"

SCIENTIFIC MATTERS

26. *n.* (chemistry) The symbol for the element yttrium
    in the periodic table.

27. *n.* (electronics) Admittance.

28. *n.* (biology) Tyrosine, an amino acid.

29. *n.* (biology) A male sex chromosome.
    *The Y chromosome is one of the two chromosomes
    that determine sex; the other is called the X chro-
    mosome. The Y chromosome appears only in males;
    it is associated with the development of male sex
    characteristics, such as the testes. During fertil-
    ization of the ovum, if a Y chromosome is paired
    with an X chromosome, the fetus will develop into
    a male. If two X chromosomes are paired, the fetus
    will develop into a female. The Y chromosome is so-
    called because its shape is markedly different from
    the other 45 chromosomes, which all resemble the X
    chromosome.* —World Book

MISCELLANEOUS

30. *n.* Any spoken sound represented by the letter.
    *The sound vibration of the consonant Y means
    "awareness."* —Joseph E. Rael, *Tracks of Dancing
    Light: A Native American Approach to Understand-
    ing Your Name*

31. *n.* The twenty-fifth letter of the alphabet.
    *Y's career as a member of the Roman alphabet has
    been more checkered than that of any other letter.*
    —Alexander Humez, *A B C Et Cetera*

32. *n.* The twenty-fifth section in a piece of music.

33. *n.* A word designated Y.
    If you find yourself in X situation, try using Y word.
    —Kate Deimling, in a Verbatim journal review of
    the book *They Have a Word for It*

34. *n.* A golf swing position involving an "arm-shoulder triangle."
As you grip the club directly out in front of the body, the arm-shoulder triangle might be accurately described as a lowercase letter y. The left arm and club shaft form the straight-line side of the y, while the right arm approaches the left arm and club shaft at an angle. — Michael McTeigue, *The Keys to the Effortless Golf Swing: Curing Your Hit Impulse in Seven Simple Lessons*

35. *n.* Y connection: an electrical junction device in which one wire carrying an incoming signal is split so that the signal continues down two outgoing wires.

36. *n.* Y front: a style of men's jockey briefs with overlapping flaps in the front.
The first ever Y-front commercial aired in America was on The Tonight Show *in 1958. Host Jack Paar found the pants so hilarious that his laughter strung a Y-front endorsement out for two minutes instead of the allowed 30 seconds. The next day they sold out across the country.* —Ryan Parry, "A Brief History of Y-fronts," *The Daily Mirror*, August 16, 2004

37. *n.* Y junction: an intersection of three roads.
They came to a Y-junction. She looked both ways. To the right was a long straight passageway, going into darkness. It probably led to the laboratory, she thought. To the left was a much shorter section of tunnel, with stairs at the end. She went left. —Michael Crichton, *The Lost World*

38. *n.* Y level: a surveyor's telescope whose supports are Y-shaped.

39. *n.* Y ligament: a ligament with two branches extending from the spine to the femur; the iliofemoral ligament.

40. *n.* Y point: the neutral point on a three-phase electrical circuit.

41. *n.* Y tile: a Y-shaped drainage or gutter tile.

42. *n.* Y track: a railroad switch.
[T]he track workers have come across all manner of humanity in the subway over the years. Like the homeless man who liked to sit at the Y in the tracks, in a lawn chair, with a battery-powered light, reading The Wall Street Journal. —Randy Kennedy, *Subwayland: Adventures in the World Beneath New York*

43. *n.* Y-Tube: a radiant hot-water heating system consisting of aluminum tubes with three fins, which maximize surface area for heat dissipation. The three fins form a Y-shaped cross-section.

FOREIGN MEANINGS

44. *conj.* (Spanish) And, as in *Maria y Juan*, "Maria and Juan."

FACTS AND FIGURES

45. *Y* is known as the "Letter of Pythagoras." **Pythagoras, a Greek philosopher and mathematician of the 6th century B.C., used *Y* as a symbol of the divergent paths of virtue and vice.**

Z IN PRINT AND PROVERB

1. (in literature) *"In the purple distance neatly scripted alphabet vultures with Zs for eyes soared in the thermals swirling over and around an alphabet volcano spewing what appeared to be incomplete, fractured sentences and clustered gobs of words that were half submerged in a river of blood red lava."* —George C. Chesbro, *The Language of Cannibals*

2. (in literature) *"Thou whoreson zed! / thou unnecessary letter!"* —William Shakespeare, *King Lear*, II.ii.65.

3. (in literature) *Z Was Zapped* is the name of a 1987 play in twenty-six acts, by Chris Van Allsburg.

4. (in literature) As a high level of thought, reached via the near-genius ability to repeat every letter of the alphabet from A to Z accurately in order: *"How many men in a thousand million, he asked himself, reach Z after all? . . . One in a generation. Is he to be blamed then if he is not that one?"* —Virginia Woolf, *To the Lighthouse*

5. (in literature) As a letter of the alphabet with dynamic energy: *"[T]he letter Z has a dynamic energy to it, and it is the diagonal line connecting the two short horizontal lines that creates that energy."* —Brenda Tharp, *Creative Nature & Outdoor Photography*

6. (in literature) *"Z is lightning, the sign of God."* —Victor Hugo, quoted in *ABZ* by Mel Gooding

7. (in film) *Alphabet Zelda* is a 2004 short film by Eva Saks about a little girl's hunt for the letter Z. The film was created for the *Sesame Street* television program.

8. **(in film)** Mind-altering radiation in the 2001 film *The Caveman's Valentine.*
   [T]he solution makes perfect sense to a man who is wracked by "brain typhoons" caused by yellow "Y-beams" and green "Z-beams" emanating from the spires of the Chrysler Building. Somewhere inside that landmark, a mysterious evil mastermind named Cornelius Gould Stuyvesant tracks and torments our hapless hero. —CrankyCritic.com

9. *n.* A written representation of the letter.
   Outside a late-spring rain was falling, and the Crown Z Mill, as we left it in our wake, was doing its best to turn the gray dawn grayer. —David James Duncan, The Brothers K

10. *n.* A device, such as a printer's type, for reproducing the letter.

ASLEEP AMID FLOWERS

11. *n.* Sleep.
    "It's going to be a long night, men. You wanna catch some z's, work it out with your buddy." —Al Franken, Rush Limbaugh Is a Big Fat Idiot

12. *n.* A buzzing sound, as from an insect.
    Flying bee z z z z. —Sue Lloyd, "Jolly Phonics" Workbook 5

STAYING IN PLACE

13. *n.* The third in order or class when x is made the first.
    The first of these major parts is divided into three sections, of which the first considers X, the second considers Y, and the third considers Z. —Charles Van Doren, How to Read a Book

14. *n.* Something arbitrarily designated Z (e.g., a person, place, or other thing).
    It is a gift, from X, Y, Z, to the Hospital. —Lewis Carroll, *Sylvie and Bruno Concluded*

15. *n.* The twenty-sixth in a series.
    Nicknamed Scheme Z because it was the twenty-sixth alternative explored for the crossing, its engineers and Salvucci hoped it would be the last. —Thomas P. Hughes, *Rescuing Prometheus: Four Monumental Projects That Changed the Modern World*

MISCELLANEOUS

16. *n.* The end, as in "from A to Z."
    "They have fallen past Z," said old Johanna. "They have disappeared from the human alphabet."
    —John Irving, *The World According to Garp.* Here the speaker is giving a letter rating to a displeasing establishment.
    "That's me to the letter Z." Daniel showed all his pink gums in a wide smile. Of course he could not read and knew of the letter Z only by repute, which made Hal smile inwardly. —Wilbur A. Smith, *Monsoon Scientific advance was once thought of as a march toward Z, but the twentieth century spoiled the sequence. Instead of moving to the next letter, ideas kept cropping up that required a whole different alphabet. The universe turned out to be fundamentally unknowable in some of the areas we most wanted to learn about. Z faded out to infinity.*
    —Charles Wohlforth, *The Whale and the Supercomputer: On the Northern Front of Climate Change*

17. *n.* Any spoken sound represented by the letter.
    The sound vibration of the consonant Z means "as above, so below, heaven and earth." —Joseph E.

Rael, *Tracks of Dancing Light: A Native American Approach to Understanding Your Name*

18. *n.* The twenty-sixth letter of the alphabet.
    [T]he low craft and chicanery characteristic of z.
    —William H. Gass, *The Tunnel*
    In 1969 [contemporary artist Don] Driver held an exhibition in which the title of every work began with the letter Z. That choice of letter seems even more perfect three decades later.... [H]is best works, in their absurd beauty, are still most at home at the far end of the alphabet. —Justin Paton, "The Alphabet According to Don Driver"
    If she could be any letter of the alphabet she wanted to be, I said, which letter would she choose. The answer she gave me was so faint that I had to bend down to hear. It was the letter Z. She wanted to be the last *letter, in other words.* —Frederick Buechner, *Telling Secrets*

19. *n.* Someone called Z.
    Dr. Z had made his dubious contribution—and he was gone. —Oscar Levant, *The Memoirs of an Amnesiac*
    Bernstein printed the letter Z on the top sheet of a blue memo pad; X had been retired with the Bookkeeper. "My boss calls it a whitewash," said Z. —Carl Bernstein, *All the President's Men*

20. *n.* Something having the shape of a Z.
    Uncle Willie used to sit like a giant black Z. —Maya Angelou, *I Know Why the Caged Bird Sings*
    I awoke a little before seven, cuddled up to my wife Lillian, who was accordioned up into a Z in the bed beside me. —Luke Rhinehart, *The Dice Man*

21. *n.* An unknown thing.

22. *n.* A medieval Roman numeral for 2,000.

23. *n.* The twenty-sixth section in a piece of music.

24. *n.* Z bar: a metal construction unit with a Z-shaped cross-section.

25. *n.* Z beam: a metal or wood construction unit with a Z-shaped cross-section.
New z-beam construction offers an unparalleled frame structure. —Dave Mattern, HorseTrainerWorld.com

26. *n.* Z crank: a crank shaped like the letter Z.
Z cranks are manufactured to tighter specs than most American made cranks. —"Twin Turbo Zs of Dallas," ttzd.com

27. *n.* Z twist: a type of yarn that has been spun clockwise so that the slope of fibers resembles a Z.
Nurdane could feel them watching her work, studying the turn of her fingers, the way her left hand fed the wool into the spindle while her right rotated it clockwise, making a Z-twist with the yarn. —Holly Payne, *The Virgin's Knot*

28. *n.* A European automotive lamp with a Z-shaped light pattern.
I have had night vision problems for years and have, in the past, upgraded my sealed beam headlights to bulb type "Z" beams. —Charlie S., RealCarAudio.com

SCIENTIFIC MATTERS

29. *n.* In the Cartesian coordinate system, the depth axis of a three-dimensional space.
It is common to label the axis representing the width of a three-dimensional space with the letter X, the height axis with the letter Y, and the depth axis

with the letter Z. —Isaac Victor Kerlow, *The Art of 3-D Computer Animation and Effects, Third Edition*

30. *n.* (physics) Atomic number.

31. *n.* (electronics) Impedance.
    Sometimes, the capital letter Z is used in place of the word "impedance" in general discussions [of electronics]. —Stan Gibilisco, *Teach Yourself Electricity and Electronics*

32. *n.* (astronomy) Zenith distance.

33. *n.* (astronomy) Redshift.
    Astronomers use the letter z to denote redshift. —Roger A. Freedman, *Universe*

34. *n.* The vertical component of the total intensity of a magnetic field, measured in units of nanoTesla. The Earth's magnetic field intensity is roughly between 25,000 and 65,000 nT.

35. *n.* A hypothetical explosive, vastly more powerful than the A-bomb and H-bomb.
    [W]e could never be certain that a future device, let us call it a Z-bomb, with an even stronger blast, would destroy the beaker. —Peter Mitchell, *Psychology of Childhood*

𝓛